D0507359

Weber Presents:

COMMAND OF THE GRILL

A SALUTE TO STEAK™

A COLLECTION OF RECIPES TO BENEFIT CHARITIES THAT SUPPORT MARINES

weber

Produced by:
  rabble+rouser, inc.
Consultants:
  Jamie Purviance
  Susie Landau Finch
Food photography:
  Tim Turner Studio
Color imaging and in-house prepress:
  Weber Creative Services
Front cover illustration:
  Shum Prats
Photography credits:
  Michael Stevens: pages 4, 20-22, 26-28, 32-34, 38-40, 44-46, 74-76
  Bob Gruen: page 6
  Brendan Mattingly: pages 8-9
  Tim Turner Studio: pages 14, 19
  Michael McCreary: page 25
  Courtesy of Patrick Tenore Sr.: page 31
  Courtesy of George Jones: page 37
  Courtesy of Bum Phillips: page 43
  © 2006 PGA Tour (top photo), courtesy of Lee Trevino (bottom photo): page 49
  Susan McSpadden: pages 50-52
  Courtesy of the National Basketball Retired Players Association: page 55
  Fred Greaves: pages 56-58
  Courtesy of Focus on Sport/Getty Images: page 61
  Robert Kratzke: pages 62-64
  Courtesy of Wilford Brimley: page 67
  Sue Jarrett: pages 68-70
  Courtesy of Art Donovan Jr.: page 73
  Courtesy of Dan Lauria: page 79
Used with permission.

Weber-Stephen Products Co.:
  Mike Kempster Sr., Executive Vice President
  Sherry Bale, Director, News Media Relations

© 2006 Weber-Stephen Products Co. Weber, the kettle configuration and the kettle silhouette are registered trademarks; Command of the Grill is a trademark; all of Weber-Stephen Products Co., 200 East Daniels Road, Palatine, Illinois 60067 USA. All rights reserved.

Wish-Bone and Lawry's are registered trademarks of Unilever Supply Chain, Inc., Clinton, Connecticut; Dale's is a registered trademark of Dale's Sauces, Inc., Birmingham, Alabama; Morton & Bassett is a registered trademark of Morton Gothelf, Novato, California; Jack Daniels is a registered trademark of Jack Daniels Properties, Inc., San Rafael, California; Kikkoman is a registered trademark of Kikkoman International, Inc., San Francisco, California; Goya and Sazon Goya are registered trademarks of Goya Foods, Inc., Seacacus, New Jersey; Crown Royal is a registered trademark of Diageo North America, Inc., Norwalk, Connecticut; McCormick is a registered trademark of McCormick & Company Incorporated, Sparks, Maryland; Corona is a registered trademark of Cerveceria Modelo, S.A. de C.V., Mexico, D.F., Mexico; Dos Equis is a registered trademark of CCM IP S. A., Lausanne, Switzerland; Dr. Pepper is a registered trademark of Dr. Pepper/Seven Up, Inc., Plano, Texas; A.1. is a registered trademark of Kraft Foods Holdings, Northfield, Illinois; and Mrs. Dash is a registered trademark of Alberto-Culver Company, Melrose Park, Illinois.

No part of this book may be reproduced in any form including, but not limited to, storage in a retrieval system or transmission in any form or by any means, electronic, mechanical, photocopied, scanned, downloaded, recorded, or otherwise, without prior written permission.

10 9 8 7 6 5 4 3 2 1

ISBN 0-9778291-0-3
Library of Congress Control Number: 2006923730

Printed in the United States of America by FCL Graphics, Inc.

For additional copies of *Command of the Grill. A Salute to Steak*™, visit our Web site at www.commandofthegrill.com or call 1-800-446-1071.

Neither the U.S. Government, the U.S. Marine Corps, nor participating Marine Corps personnel endorse or promote this product, company, and named charities.

The Story of This Book

It all started over a burger and a beer. John McCann and Susan Maruyama, two of my Weber colleagues, had stopped for dinner at Chumley's in New York City after working a long day at a trade show. Susan's daughter, Michi, was working at Chumley's at the time. She warned John and Susan that it might "get a little nuts" in the bar because it was Fleet Week. Fleet Week is an annual event in which Navy and Coast Guard ships as well as ships from all over the world dock in the harbors of New York. Thousands of sailors and Marines file off the boats in a steady stream and flood the streets of New York. It's a time when the fine young men and women who protect our country can relax and have some fun and the city welcomes them with open arms.

Sure enough, halfway through their meal, a very large group of Marines descended on Chumley's. Within minutes the bar was packed. Over the course of the evening, Susan and John had the great pleasure of meeting a high-ranking general who is not only an inspirational patriot, but also a self-avowed grilling fanatic. They immediately bonded over our shared passion for our country and a good grilled steak. The General recounted stories of how Marines under his command used grilling as an outlet to relax and de-stress from the very demanding and often times, dangerous jobs.

Susan and John suggested that perhaps there was something Weber could do to support the troops, like a big grill-off during Fleet Week 2006. The General suggested a meeting with the officers who facilitate the Marine participation in Fleet Week. Several weeks later, we all met to discuss the merit of the idea.

Before long, we had conjured up a grand idea: create a series of grilling competitions on Marine Corps installations around the country with a big-bang final competition during Fleet Week 2006. And since we had published several best-selling cookbooks, Weber decided to use the recipes gathered from the competition to create a cookbook produced and sold by Weber with all proceeds going to charities that support Marines and their families.

With the tremendous help of Major Andersen, Gunnery Sergeant Jamison, and support from the USMC New York City Public Affair's Office (PAO), Nancy Pasternack, Headquarters Marine Corps, and the local PAO and Marine Corps Community Services staffs, we were holding grilling competitions at Marine Corps installations by late summer. In total, just under 100 men and women squared off over charcoal grills in competitions held at 10 installations across the country.

It was both a pleasure and a privilege to meet the fine young men and women serving our country along the way. Their recipes were delicious and their personal stories engaging. We're happy to be able to bring them to you in this book. We're also happy to share recipes from some notable former Marines like Ed McMahon and Lee Trevino, who, when they learned of this fundraiser, generously offered up their owned grilled steak recipes to support the cause.

Inside you will also learn about the very important charities you are supporting with your donation and what they are doing to help the men and women wounded in service, as well as the families of those who have fallen in the line of duty. The work they are doing is truly worthy of a salute.

Sincerely,

Mike

Mike Kempster Sr.
Executive Vice President, Weber-Stephen Products Co.

To read more about the Command of the Grill™ competition, visit www.commandofthegrill.com.

TABLE OF CONTENTS

Foreword

Chumley's, a landmark "speakeasy" in the West Village of New York City, still has no sign over the entrance. In fact, if you do not know what it is, you would think you were walking into someone's front door rather than an historical pub. It has been a gathering place since the early 1900s and it was there that the idea for this book was born.

When we sat down with Mike Kempster and Susan Maruyama to discuss how Weber could show their appreciation to the Marines for sacrifices they have made for our great nation, we never expected such an overwhelming effort.

It is obvious that the people of Weber and the other contributors to this monumental endeavor genuinely care about what they are doing. They have jumped into this with both feet and all of their hearts and it is greatly appreciated.

Semper Fidelis!
Major David C. Andersen
Gunnery Sergeant John S. Jamison Jr.
United States Marine Corps
New York City Public Affairs

Filet Mignon Steaks with Béarnaise Sauce

FROM
MAJOR DAVID C. ANDERSEN, USMC NEW YORK CITY PUBLIC AFFAIRS

6   filet mignon steaks, about 8 ounces each and
        1 inch thick
        Extra virgin olive oil
1-1/2   tablespoons finely chopped fresh tarragon
1   teaspoon kosher salt
1/2   teaspoon freshly ground black pepper

Sauce
2   tablespoons tarragon vinegar
1   tablespoon minced shallots
1/4   teaspoon freshly ground black pepper
3   large egg yolks
1/2   cup (1 stick) unsalted butter, melted and
        cooled to room temperature
2   tablespoons fresh lemon juice
1   teaspoon finely chopped fresh tarragon
1/2   teaspoon kosher salt
        Ground cayenne pepper (to taste)

1. Lightly coat the steaks on both sides with oil. Season evenly with the tarragon, salt, and pepper. Let the steaks stand at room temperature for 20 to 30 minutes before grilling. Meanwhile, make the sauce.

2. In a small skillet mix the vinegar, shallots, and black pepper with 1 tablespoon of water. Bring to a boil and cook until almost all the liquid has evaporated. Allow to cool. Whisk the egg yolks in the upper section of a double boiler. Add the shallot mixture and 2 tablespoons of water to the eggs and whisk again. Pour 1 to 2 inches of hot water in the bottom section of the double boiler and put the upper section on top. Whisking the egg mixture often, bring the water in the bottom section to a simmer. Do not let the water boil. When the egg mixture is as thick as heavy cream, drizzle the melted butter very, very slowly into the egg mixture, whisking constantly. After all the butter has been incorporated, remove the double boiler from the heat. Add the remaining sauce ingredients. Whisk again. Set the upper section of the double boiler aside while you grill the steaks.

3. Grill the steaks over **direct high** heat (500°F to 550°F) until cooked to desired doneness, 6 to 8 minutes for medium-rare, turning once. Remove the steaks from the grill and spoon the sauce over the top. Serve warm.

Makes 6 servings

T-Bone Steaks with Cajun Spices

FROM
GUNNERY SERGEANT JOHN S. JAMISON JR., USMC NEW YORK CITY PUBLIC AFFAIRS

Rub
1-1/2   teaspoons kosher salt
1   teaspoon light brown sugar
1   teaspoon granulated garlic
1   teaspoon paprika
1   teaspoon dried oregano
1/2   teaspoon freshly ground black pepper
1/4   teaspoon ground cayenne pepper

4   T-bone steaks, 12 to 16 ounces each and
        about 1 inch thick
        Olive oil

1. In a small bowl mix the rub ingredients.

2. Coat the steaks lightly on both sides with olive oil. Massage the rub onto both sides of each steak. Let the steaks stand at room temperature for 20 to 30 minutes before grilling.

3. With the lid closed, grill the steaks over **direct medium-high** heat (450°F to 500°F) until cooked to desired doneness, 8 to 10 minutes for medium-rare, turning once or twice. (If flare-ups occur, move the steaks temporarily over *indirect medium-high* heat.) Remove from the grill and let rest for 2 to 3 minutes before carving. Serve warm.

Makes 4 to 6 servings

CHARITIES

Injured Marine Semper Fi Fund

Serving Those Who Preserve Our Freedom

Since September 11, 2001, United States Marines have been on the front line in the War Against Terror. Whether fighting wars or winning the peace, Marines serve their country and their Corps with courage and commitment. Sometimes that service results in catastrophic injuries. When serious injuries occur, the Injured Marine Semper Fi Fund is there to help.

The Need

Wounded Marines and sailors are given the finest medical care available, but it is their families that provide the emotional component for healing. These families share the pain and burden of recovery, but few have the resources to get them through this stressful time. They are not prepared for the personal and financial disruption that occurs when they drop everything to be with their loved one through long months of hospitalization and rehabilitation. Often, they must take leave from their jobs without pay, and incur expenses for travel, lodging, child care, and other necessities. Their need is genuine, and immediate.

The IMSFF was created to respond to this need.

Our Mission

The Injured Marine Semper Fi Fund provides financial assistance to injured Marines and other service members injured while assigned to Marine forces. The goal is to alleviate the financial burden placed on the family so that their focus can be on their loved one's recovery. If the mother of a wounded Marine needs help with travel expenses to be with her son or daughter, the Semper Fi Fund is there. If the wife of an injured Marine falls behind on a mortgage payment because she left work to be with her husband at the hospital, the Semper Fi Fund is there. If a wounded Marine, whose sight was impaired from an RPG blast, needs a special magnifier, the Semper Fi Fund is there.

"Semper Fi" means "Always Faithful." That is our pledge to the heroic Marines who have been injured while protecting our nation.

The Fund

The Injured Marine Semper Fi Fund was established in May 2004. A nurse at Camp Pendleton Naval Hospital, whose husband was deployed to Iraq, saw first hand the needs of those returning from battle. She brought together a group of Marine Corps spouses to implement a plan to give financial grants and needed equipment to injured Marines and their families. In the summer of 2004, General Alfred Gray, 29th Commandant of the Marine Corps, two retired general officers, and a retired sergeant major joined them.

The Fund works closely with Marine Corps, Navy, Army and VA hospitals nationwide to identify and assess the needs of specific families. Once a family has been identified, they are given a grant application. Upon submitting a completed application, the case is reviewed by a Fund caseworker and then referred to a committee for approval. Typically, assistance is provided in less than 72 hours from submission and there is no expectation of repayment.

To date, the Fund has provided more than $3 million in assistance, thanks to the overwhelming generosity of donors from across America.

www.semperfifund.org

Wounded Warrior Project

The mission of the Wounded Warrior Project (WWP) is to raise public awareness and enlist the public's aid for the needs of severely injured service men and women, to help severely injured service members to aid and assist each other, and to provide unique, direct programs and services to meet their needs.

WWP accomplishes this mission by providing programs and services to severely injured active service members and their families during the critical time between their initial rehabilitation while on active duty and their eventual transition to civilian life. WWP employs staff with over 55 years of combined experience in providing direct services to active duty service members and disabled veterans, including benefits counseling, representation before the department of veterans affairs, bringing public attention to the needs of wounded service members, and advocating for regulatory and statutory changes beneficial to veterans and active duty service members.

There are many military service organizations that provide services to active duty service members and their families, and many veteran service organizations that provide services and opportunities for fraternal interaction to veterans upon their discharge from service. However, few organizations devote their resources to assisting the severely wounded during this critical period. WWP fills this vital, unmet need, bringing comfort, support, and aid to severely injured service members and their families during this challenging time in their lives.

The Wounded Warrior Project was founded on the principle that veterans are our nation's greatest citizens. The WWP seeks to assist those men and women of our armed forces who have been severely injured during the conflicts in Iraq, Afghanistan, and other locations around the world. Many of the injuries are traumatic amputations, gunshot wounds, burns and blast injuries that will retire these brave warriors from military service.

At the Wounded Warrior Project we provide programs and services designed to ease the burdens of the wounded and their families, aid in the recovery process, and smooth the transition back to civilian life.

Our work begins at the bedside of the severely wounded, where we provide comfort items and necessities, counseling, and support for families. We help to speed rehabilitation and recovery through adaptive sports and recreation programs, raising patients' morale, and exposing them to the endless possibilities of life after an injury. Finally, we provide a support mechanism for those who have returned home, providing outreach and advocacy on issues like debt and disability payments that will affect their families' future.

We cannot restore the lost limbs, but we can help restore to our Wounded Warriors their dignity by ensuring that they are not forgotten.

www.woundedwarriorproject.org

Fisher House

A Fisher House is a "home away from home" for families of patients receiving medical care at major military and VA medical centers. As of this printing, there are 35 Fisher Houses located on 18 military installations and eight VA medical centers, with another three houses under construction. The program began in 1990 and has offered more than two million days of lodging to more than 75,000 families.

Fisher House Foundation donated Fisher Houses to the U. S. Government. They have full-time salaried managers, but depend on volunteers and voluntary support to enhance daily operations and program expansion.

Through the generosity of the American public, the foundation has expanded its programs to meet the needs of our service men and women who have been wounded in the Global War on Terrorism. The foundation uses donated frequent flyer miles to provide airline travel to reunite families of the wounded and to enable our wounded heroes to go home to convalesce. The foundation also sponsors a service for creating personal web journals on the Internet to keep family and friends up to date during the hospitalization of a loved one. Called "CaringBridge," the service is free for military and veterans' families.

Families of service men and women hospitalized due to their service in Iraq or Afghanistan do not pay to stay at a Fisher House, and the foundation helps cover the cost of alternative housing when the Fisher Houses are full.

For further information about these programs, to find out about volunteering, or to make a tax-deductible gift, go to their web site at: *www.fisherhouse.org*

You can also obtain information by writing them at: Fisher House Foundation, Inc., 1401 Rockville Pike, Suite 600, Rockville, Maryland 20852. Phone: (888) 294-8560. Email: info@fisherhouse.org.

Marine Corps-Law Enforcement Foundation

Marine Corps - Law Enforcement Foundation

Mission: To encourage the spiritual, moral, intellectual and physical development of children through education.

This Foundation was formed in February 1995 by former Marines and law enforcement personnel who strongly believe that our nation's most precious resource is its youth.

The recent war in Iraq has certainly illuminated America's commitment to freedom. We are reminded that freedom is not free. The price is great. No one knows that better than the left-behind sons and daughters of America's fallen heroes.

Through continuous support of our donors, we have distributed aid with a value of more than $24 million to eligible children. This assistance was primarily rendered to children of Marines or Federal law enforcement personnel who were killed on duty or died under extraordinary circumstances while serving our country at home or abroad. These funds enable us to provide these children with scholarships for their higher education. When a child of a United States Marine is afflicted with a physical or mental disability and requires special medical equipment or tutoring, our Foundation may grant financial assistance to that family if their personal insurance does not cover the complete cost of treatment for this child.

In addition to the regular program, our Foundation decided to support all American Forces and also Coalition Forces in the invasion of Iraq and taking of Baghdad from 3 March 2003 to 16 July 2003. In the past, the Foundation also included in our program the children who lost a parent from all agencies killed in the murderous attack on the Pentagon. We also decided to go back and give our bonds to children who lost a parent on the USS Cole; the children of the Air Force personnel killed at Khobar Towers; and, with great honor, the twelve children who lost their parent on the space shuttle Columbia disaster.

This assistance has had a positive, life-changing effect on many, many children. We are thankful for the commitment and support of our many members and volunteers. Because of their dedication, no administrative costs of any type are charged to our Foundation. One hundred percent of the donations received is used to fund programs for the children we serve.

www.mclef.org

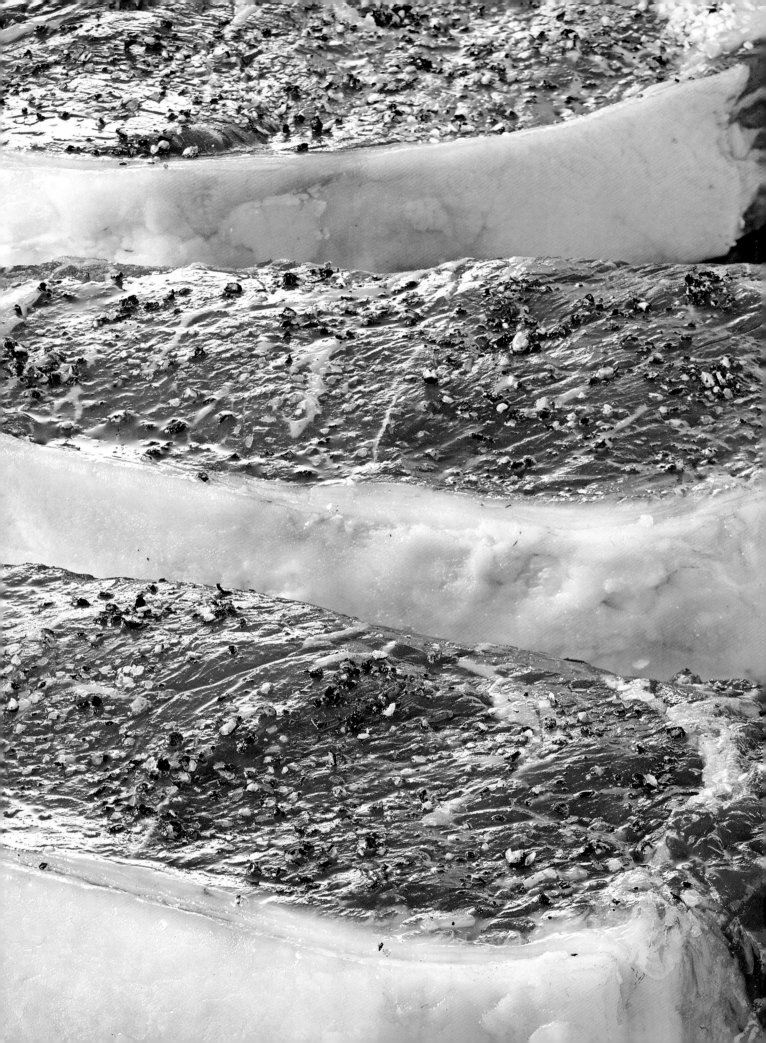

Steak Boot Camp

FOR 15 YEARS, WEBER HAS SURVEYED CONSUMERS ACROSS THE COUNTRY TO FIND OUT WHAT AMERICA LOVES TO GRILL. WHAT TOPS THE LIST? STEAK. SURE, BURGERS, HOT DOGS, AND BRATS ARE ALL DELICIOUS ON THE GRILL, BUT NOTHING MAKES A GRILLER'S HEART PALPITATE LIKE A BIG, JUICY, PERFECTLY COOKED STEAK.

A GOOD STEAK IS ONE OF LIFE'S SIMPLE PLEASURES, BUT GRILLING IT TO PERFECTION TAKES A LITTLE KNOWLEDGE AND SKILL. BUT ONCE YOU'VE GOT IT DOWN, YOU'LL BE ABLE TO GRILL STEAKS EVERY BIT AS GOOD AS WHAT YOU'D GET AT A HIGH-PRICED STEAK JOINT. JUST FOLLOW THESE TIPS AND TECHNIQUES AND YOU'LL BE LARGE AND IN CHARGE IN NO TIME WHEN IT COMES TO STEAK.

BEEF UP YOUR STEAK KNOWLEDGE

Ever stood in front of the meat counter pondering the grades of beef and what they mean? You're not alone. Here's the scoop.

There are eight beef grades specified by the United States Department of Agriculture (USDA), four of which are commonly found in the butcher's case. Meat grading is voluntary, but most producers participate for the consumer's benefit. The grades are a good gauge of what you can expect in terms of flavor and tenderness. Grades are based on the animal's age (younger is better) and the marbling in the muscle (flecks of fat visible in the meat).

Prime beef is the best you can buy – only 2 percent of beef earns this title for its abundance of marbling. Most Prime meat is sold to fine restaurants, but you can find it at a good butcher. When you want a really fantastic steak, hunt down some Prime. It's unparalleled in taste and juiciness.

Certified Angus Beef™ is not actually a USDA grade; it is a trademarked designation reserved for meat that meets strict standards for flavor, juiciness, and tenderness. Only 8 percent of beef meets this standard. Many people prefer it over other grades and the marbling can be as rich as with Prime. It's widely available in the grocery stores and meat counters and is an affordable alternative to Prime.

Choice is the second best and most widely available USDA grade of beef. The meat comes from fairly young cattle and has moderate to small amounts of marbling. Choice is an excellent value for the grill.

Select grade beef is leaner and less expensive than Choice grade. Because it has minimal marbling, it tends to be tougher and less flavorful. Unless you plan to marinate your steak, you are better off opting for a Choice cut for the grill.

IT GETS BETTER WITH AGE

There are two types of aging for beef: dry aging and wet aging. Both make the meat more tender and flavorful. In the process of dry aging, beef is hung unwrapped in a refrigerated cooler for 3 to 6 weeks. During this time two things happen: the muscles lose up to 10 percent of their weight from moisture evaporation, concentrating the beef flavor in the meat, and the fibers in the muscle break down, making the meat more tender. Wet-aged beef is sealed in airtight bags, so there's no moisture loss. Wet-aged or dry-aged, it's a matter of personal preference, but both enhance the flavor of steak.

GET THE DRILL DOWN

Once you've selected just the right steak, there are seven simple steps for pulling a perfect steak off the grill every time. Follow them and your steaks will be worthy of a salute.

1. **Give it a rest.** Prior to grilling, remove your steak from the refrigerator and allow it to stand at room temperature for 20 to 30 minutes. Why? First, the fibers in the meat relax, producing more tenderness after cooking. Second, a properly rested steak will cook faster than a cold one, which means less moisture will be lost.

2. **Trim it down.** You will want to leave a small layer of fat around the edges of your steak to add flavor, but don't overdo it. Trim all but 1/4 inch of fat around the outer edge. Any more than that could lead to flare-ups.

3. **Oil it up.** That's right. It doesn't seem necessary to oil a steak with lots of marbling, but it helps prevent sticking. No need to slather it on; a very light coat of extra virgin olive oil will do. Avoid oiling the cooking grate. Oil on a hot cooking grate by itself burns very quickly, creating unpleasant bitter flavors.

4. **Sprinkle on the salt.** If you are grilling a steak and not using a recipe, salt the steak 20 to 30 minutes before it goes on the grill. It will begin to mingle with the juices, which helps in browning the steak when it is one the grill. But salting a steak too far ahead of time can be risky because the salt crystals have a tendency to draw moisture out of the meat over hours and hours. Kosher salt with its larger crystals and pure flavors is the salt of choice because it is less likely to dissolve completely and lose its individual character.

5. **Keep an eye on things.** Unless it is a very thick cut, most steaks require less than 10 minutes total time on the grill, so refrain from multi-tasking when the steak is on. (Consult the grilling guide on page 19 for suggested cooking times.) Usually, you'll want to start by searing the steak over direct high heat. Make sure the grill is good and hot before placing the steak on the grill. This is critical for a good sear. After you've seared the steak, continue cooking over direct or indirect heat, depending on the thickness of the steak. Cuts under 1-1/4 inches thick cook quickly and can be done entirely over direct heat. Larger cuts require more cooking time and are best finished over indirect heat. While you are grilling, remember to keep the lid down. It will keep the heat up and speed up the cooking time.

6. **Forego the fork and step away from the knife.** Meat forks are intended to help lift large roasts off the grate, not for flipping steaks or poking your meat while it cooks. Doing so will cause precious juices to escape, which will dry out your steak. Turn your steak with a set of tongs instead. When you think it's done, resist the urge to cut into it with a knife to check. Again, you'll lose some of that juicy goodness. A better plan is to set a timer when you put the steak on the grill. It takes the guesswork—and the stress—out of cooking a perfect steak.

7. **Give it a rest—again.** After you remove the steak from the grill, allow it to stand at room temperature for 3 to 5 minutes. This allows the juices that were pushed to the center of the meat by the heat of the grill to migrate back to all parts of the steak so you have juiciness throughout.

A WORD ABOUT DONENESS

Everyone likes their steak cooked just so. The USDA recommends that steak is cooked to at least medium-rare, which by their definition means an internal temperature of 145°F. Many steak aficionados will find this temperature too high. You can enjoy beef at a safe 145°F, but if you like your meat juicier, know that it comes with some risk. In order to reach 145°F as your finished temperature, remove your steak from the grill at 135°F to 140°F. Stopping short allows for carry-over cooking, which means the temperature continues to rise up to 10°F as the meat rests (the larger the cut, the higher it will rise).

HOW TO GET GREAT GRILL MARKS

Ever wonder how they get those fabulous crosshatched steak marks at the best steak houses? Here's how to do it in your own backyard.

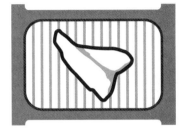

SEAR

Preheat the grill and set it up for direct high heat (charcoal grills can be set up with medium heat on one side and high heat on the other). Place the steak over direct high heat. Allow the meat to sear for 1 to 2 minutes, depending on the thickness.

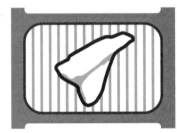

ROTATE 90°

With a wide spatula or tongs, lift and rotate the steak a quarter turn (do not flip it). Sear for 1 to 2 minutes.

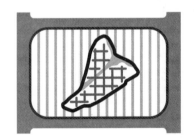

FLIP & FINISH

Lift the steak with the spatula or tongs and flip it over. There is no need to rotate the steak on the second side and create another set of crosshatched marks, because only the first side will show on the plate. Cuts that cook in less than 8 minutes can be finished over direct high heat. For large cuts with a total cooking time of more than 8 minutes, place over direct medium heat to finish the steak. Grill to desired doneness.

KNOW YOUR CUTS

All these cuts are particularly well suited for the grill—tender, juicy, and flavorful.

Porterhouse: This monster cut is taken from the large end of the short loin. It can weigh in at 2+ pounds. It's the perfect steak for sharing because it's actually two steaks in one. On one side of the bone you have a filet mignon, and the other is a strip steak.

T-Bone: Smaller than the porterhouse, the T-bone is cut from the narrow end of the short loin, so the section of filet mignon is smaller. The favorite of many steak enthusiasts who like the flavor the bone imparts.

Strip Steak: A classic steakhouse cut, the strip steak is cut from the center of the top loin. It's even better if it includes a slice of the bone. There are many regional names for this cut: New York strip, Kansas City strip, shell, Delmonico, Ambassador, hotel cut, sirloin club, and top loin. Delicious, no matter how you say it.

Rib-Eye: Many will tell you there is no better cut for the grill than the rib-eye, particularly with the bone attached (also called a rib steak). It's super tender and rich in flavor. It's cut from the muscle behind the ribs.

Filet Mignon: Cut from the trimmed tenderloin, the filet mignon is an especially tender, tasty morsel. Grill this cut quickly over high heat for best results.

Sirloin: This steak is cut from the section between the tender short loin and the tender round. Steaks are sliced from the top and the bottom; hence the names top sirloin and bottom sirloin. Most steak lovers prefer top sirloin steaks—they are more tender and juicier than bottom sirloin steaks. A dip in a good marinade helps the bottom sirloin become more tender and flavorful.

Tri-Tip: An extremely flavorful and popular cut of bottom sirloin. Because of its size, it straddles the fence between a steak and a roast. This cut is uncommon in the northern and mid-western states, but a staple in the west and southwest. Sear it first, and then grill it over indirect medium heat. Slice it thinly for sandwiches or tortilla wraps. It also goes by the names tip roast and sirloin bottom butt.

Flank Steak: One of the lowest-fat steaks, it's cut from the lean flank. It has almost no marbling, so it benefits from a good marinade to make it flavorful. Thinly sliced, it is fantastic in grilled fajitas.

Skirt Steak: Also cut from the flank, this thin and inexpensive cut should be grilled quickly over high heat. Slice it across the grain of the meat for the most tenderness.

Flatiron Steak: This flat steak, shaped like an old-fashioned iron, is cut from the shoulder. It's not common but it is gaining popularity. It tends to be a little tougher than a rib-eye or strip steak, but its flavor is deeper. Remove a thin line of gristle running down the center of the steak before grilling.

Grilling Guides

The following cuts, thicknesses, weights, and grilling times are meant to be guidelines. Cooking times are affected by altitude, wind, outside temperature, and desired doneness. Grill steaks and vegetables for the time given on the chart, or to desired doneness, turning once. Cooking times for steak are for the USDA's definition of medium-rare doneness.

VEGETABLES	APPROXIMATE GRILLING TIME
Asparagus	6 to 8 minutes direct medium
Bell pepper, whole	10 to 15 minutes direct medium
Bell/Chile pepper, 1/4-inch slices	6 to 8 minutes direct medium
Corn, husked	10 to 15 minutes direct medium
Corn, in husk	25 to 30 minutes direct medium
Garlic, whole	45 to 60 minutes indirect medium
Mushroom: shiitake or button	8 to 10 minutes direct medium
Mushroom: portabello	10 to 15 minutes direct medium
Onion: green, whole	3 to 4 minutes direct medium
Onion, 1/2-inch slices	8 to 12 minutes direct medium
Onion, halved	35 to 40 minutes indirect medium
Potato: new, halved	15 to 20 minutes direct medium
Potato, 1/2-inch slices	14 to 16 minutes direct medium
Potato, whole	45 to 60 minutes indirect medium
Squash: acorn (1 pound), halved	40 to 45 minutes indirect medium
Squash: patty pan	10 to 12 minutes direct medium
Squash: yellow, 1/2-inch slices	6 to 8 minutes direct medium
Squash: yellow, halved	6 to 10 minutes direct medium
Sweet potato, 1/4-inch slices	8 to 10 minutes direct medium
Sweet potato, whole	50 to 60 minutes indirect medium
Tomato: garden, halved	6 to 8 minutes direct medium
Tomato: plum, halved	6 to 8 minutes direct medium
Zucchini, 1/2-inch slices	6 to 8 minutes direct medium
Zucchini, halved	6 to 10 minutes direct medium

STEAK	THICKNESS/WEIGHT	APPROXIMATE GRILLING TIME
New York, porterhouse rib-eye, skirt, T-bone, tenderloin, or flatiron	1/2 inch thick	3 to 5 minutes direct high
	3/4 inch thick	5 to 7 minutes direct high
	1 inch thick	6 to 8 minutes direct high
	1-1/4 inches thick	8 to 10 minutes direct high
	1-1/2 inches thick	12 to 16 minutes; sear 8 to 10 minutes direct high, grill 4 to 6 minutes indirect high
	2 inches thick	18 to 22 minutes; sear 8 to 10 minutes direct high, grill 10 to 12 minutes indirect high
Flank steak	1-1/2 to 2 pounds, 3/4 inch thick	8 to 10 minutes direct medium-high
Sirloin steak	1 inch thick	8 to 10 minutes direct medium-high
Kabob	1 to 1-1/2 inch cubes	6 to 8 minutes direct high
Tri-tip	2 to 2-1/2 pounds	30 to 40 minutes; sear 10 minutes direct medium, grill 20 to 30 minutes indirect medium

DIRECT AND INDIRECT GRILLING

It sounds more complicated than it really is. Direct grilling is simply cooking food directly over the heat source. Indirect grilling is cooking food with the heat source to the side. It's that easy.

To set up your grill for direct cooking.

On a charcoal grill spread prepared coals evenly across the charcoal grate. On a gas grill, preheat the grill with all burners on high for 10 to 15 minutes, and then adjust the temperature, leaving the burners on directly under the food.

To set up your grill for indirect cooking.

On a charcoal grill bank prepared coals to the sides of the charcoal grate, leaving an area without coals that the food will be placed above for grilling. On a gas grill, preheat your grill on high, and then turn off the burners directly under the area where the food will be placed.

Combat Steaks

FROM

COLONEL STEWART NAVARRE
MCB CAMP PENDLETON

Colonel Stewart Navarre

The highest ranking officer in the competition, Colonel Stewart Navarre is the Chief of Staff for all Marine Corps Bases west of the Mississippi. A graduate of the US Naval Academy, Colonel Navarre has served as a Platoon Commander, a Company Commander, a Battalion Commander, and a Regimental Commander over the course of his 20-year career. He has served in Japan and Norway, and has been deployed to a number of different places, most recently Iraq.

Navarre is no stranger to the grill. He lights up the grill every weekend to cook for his wife, Yana, and their two teenage sons. He prefers charcoal to gas saying that he thinks it just tastes better.

Navarre credits his wife for his award-winning recipe. "She's the one that provides the recipes. I'll put the meat on the grill," he humbly said. She counters that his skills at the grill are equally as important as the recipe itself. "Spices are important," Mrs. Navarre said, "but the grilling is really the key and he is the commander of the grill at home, definitely."

The Colonel and his wife will travel to New York for the finals where their recipe is sure to provide some tough competition. "We would like to win," he said, "and bring a grill back to present to the Marines here at Pendleton."

Rub

1	tablespoon garlic powder
1	teaspoon salt
1/2	teaspoon freshly ground black pepper
4	bone-in rib steaks, about 10 ounces each and 1 inch thick
3	large portabello mushrooms, about 4 ounces each or 1 pound button mushrooms
1/2	cup (1 stick) butter, divided
2	teaspoons minced garlic
1/4	teaspoon salt
1/8	teaspoon freshly ground black pepper
1/4	cup red wine
1/2	cup crumbled blue or feta cheese (optional)

1. In a small bowl mix the rub ingredients.

2. Massage the rub into both sides of each steak. Let the steaks stand at room temperature for 20 to 30 minutes before grilling. Meanwhile, prepare the mushrooms.

3. Remove the mushroom stems and discard. Wipe the mushroom caps with a damp paper towel. With a teaspoon, scrape out the dark gills (if using portabello mushrooms) and discard. Cut each mushroom in half, and then cut each half crosswise into 1/2-inch slices.

4. In a 12" skillet over medium-high heat, melt 1/4 cup of the butter. Add the mushrooms and garlic, spreading the mushrooms in a single layer. Season with the salt and pepper. Cook until the mushrooms are barely tender, 4 to 5 minutes, stirring 2 or 3 times. Add the wine and cook until nearly all the wine has evaporated, about 3 minutes, stirring once. Set aside.

5. With the lid closed, grill the steaks over *direct medium-high* heat (450°F to 500°F) until cooked to desired doneness, 8 to 10 minutes for medium-rare, turning once. (If flare-ups occur, move the steaks temporarily over *indirect medium-high* heat.) Remove from the grill and let rest for 2 to 3 minutes. Meanwhile, reheat the mushrooms over medium heat, adding in the remaining 1/4 cup of butter and heating until the butter has melted. Serve the steaks warm with the mushroom and butter mixture spooned over the top. Add the crumbled cheese, if desired.

Makes 4 servings

New York Strip Shish Kabobs

FROM
SERGEANT JAMES R. CICERO JR., MCB CAMP PENDLETON
1ST RUNNER UP

4	New York strip steaks, about 12 ounces each and 1 inch thick
1	cup Wish-Bone® Italian Dressing
2	medium green bell peppers, cut into 1-inch squares
1	medium red bell pepper, cut into 1-inch squares
1	medium red onion, quartered, separated into layers, and cut into 1-inch squares
1	teaspoon garlic salt
1/2	teaspoon freshly ground black pepper

1. Trim the steaks of any excess fat and cut into 1-inch cubes. Place in a large, resealable plastic bag and pour in the dressing. Press the air out of the bag and seal tightly. Turn the bag to distribute the marinade, place in a bowl, and refrigerate for 4 to 8 hours.

2. Let the steak cubes stand at room temperature for 20 to 30 minutes before grilling. Remove the steak cubes from the bag and discard the dressing. Thread the steak cubes, bell peppers, and onion pieces onto skewers, alternating the ingredients. Season evenly with the garlic salt and pepper. With the lid closed, grill the kabobs over *direct high* heat (500°F to 550°F) until cooked to desired doneness, 6 to 8 minutes for medium-rare, turning 2 or 3 times. (If flare-ups occur, move the kabobs temporarily over *indirect high* heat.) Serve warm.

Makes 4 to 6 servings

Steak Au Poivre with Morel Mushroom Sauce

FROM
CAPTAIN KEVIN CORYELL, MCB CAMP PENDLETON
2ND RUNNER UP

4	dried morel mushrooms (about 1/4 ounce total)
1	cup dry red wine
4	rib-eye steaks, 10 to 12 ounces each and about 1 inch thick
	Extra virgin olive oil
1	tablespoon minced garlic
	Sea salt
	Cracked black peppercorns
1	tablespoon low-sodium brown gravy mix
1	tablespoon sour cream

1. In a small bowl combine the dried mushrooms and wine. Set aside until the mushrooms are soft, 45 to 60 minutes.

2. Lightly coat the steaks on both sides with oil. Rub the steaks on both sides with the garlic. Season evenly with 1 teaspoon of salt and 1 teaspoon cracked pepper. Let the steaks stand at room temperature for 20 to 30 minutes. Meanwhile, make the sauce.

3. When the mushrooms are soft, strain them in a sieve and reserve the wine in a small saucepan. Thinly slice the mushrooms. Bring the wine to a boil over medium-high heat and cook until 1/2 cup remains. Add the brown gravy mix and whisk to dissolve the lumps. Add the mushrooms. When the liquid returns to a boil, remove the saucepan from the heat and immediately whisk in the sour cream until smooth. Season with salt and pepper to taste.

4. With the lid closed, grill the steaks over *direct high* heat (500°F to 550°F) until cooked to desired doneness, 6 to 8 minutes for medium-rare, turning once. (If flare-ups occur, move the steaks temporarily over *indirect high* heat.) Let rest for 2 to 3 minutes. Meanwhile reheat the sauce over low heat. Serve the steaks warm with the sauce spooned on top.

Makes 4 servings

T-Bone Steaks with Bistro Dipping Sauce

FROM
ED McMAHON

Sauce

1/2	cup ketchup
1	tablespoon unsalted butter
2	teaspoons molasses
2	teaspoons Worcestershire sauce
2	teaspoons cider vinegar
1/2	teaspoon granulated garlic
1/4	teaspoon freshly ground black pepper

Rub

2	teaspoons kosher salt
1-1/2	teaspoons ground ancho chile powder
1/4	teaspoon ground cumin
1/4	teaspoon freshly ground black pepper
4	T-bone steaks, about 12 ounces each and 1 inch thick
2	tablespoons extra virgin olive oil

1. In a small saucepan whisk the sauce ingredients with 1/4 cup of water. Bring the sauce to a simmer over low heat and simmer gently for about 5 minutes, whisking occasionally. Set aside to cool to room temperature.

2. In a small bowl mix the rub ingredients.

3. Let the steaks stand at room temperature for 20 to 30 minutes before grilling. Lightly coat both sides of the steaks with the oil. Season them evenly with the rub, pressing the spices into the meat. Grill the steaks over *direct medium-high* heat (450°F to 500°F) until cooked to desired doneness, 8 to 10 minutes for medium-rare, turning once. (If flare-ups occur, move the steaks temporarily over *indirect medium-high* heat.) Transfer the steaks to a work surface and let rest for 3 to 5 minutes before carving. Serve warm with the dipping sauce.

Makes 4 to 6 servings

Ed McMahon

Ed McMahon has transformed the job of announcer into a star-quality role.

Known and loved for his thirty-year stint as the announcer on *The Tonight Show Starring Johnny Carson,* hosting the popular syndicated show, *Ed McMahon's Star Search,* and numerous performances as host on specials and telethons, television, and radio commercials, Mr. McMahon has become one of the most recognizable and respected men in his field.

In WWII Ed McMahon joined the Marine Corps, got his wings at Pensacola Naval Base, and became a Fighter-Pilot Instructor where he taught young students carrier landings and was a test pilot in fighters, including the sophisticated Corsair. Also serving in Korea as a Marine, McMahon flew eighty-five combat missions and rose to the rank of full Colonel.

MCB QUANTICO

Captain Robert L. Burton

May of 2006 will mark eight years of service in the Marine Corps for Captain Burton, a Tank Officer stationed at MCB Quantico. "Barbecue is my only hobby," the Mississippi native reveals. "I do it every weekend. If I'm not working or with my family, I'm barbecuing."

Captain Burton won top honors in the Quantico competition, although he admits steak is not his forte. "I always wanted to compete in a barbecue-type contest. I was just hoping to get in the top three. I use a smoker and do a lot of charcoal grilling," he reports. Burton says he's known for his smoked brisket and pork butt. "All I can say is, I have a lot of satisfied customers," he boasts.

Burton says he experimented a bit before the competition and played with different recipes. "I usually coat the meat with spicy brown mustard and then put a rub on top of that," he divulges. "It helps keep the meat tender and moist. Then I use a lot of wood chips to get plenty of smoke."

He may change his rub recipe for the final competition in New York, but for now, he's just happy to stand in the smoke a couple of times a week.

M1A1 Main Battle Steaks

FROM
Captain Robert L. Burton
MCB Quantico

Marinade

1/3	cup Dale®'s Steak Seasoning
2	tablespoons Worcestershire sauce
2	tablespoons steak sauce
1-1/2	tablespoons bourbon

4   flatiron steaks, about 8 ounces each and 1/2 inch thick

Butter

1/4	cup (1/2 stick) unsalted butter, softened
1	teaspoon minced garlic
1/2	teaspoon Morton & Bassett® Italian Seasoning
1/4	teaspoon granulated onion
1/4	teaspoon freshly ground black pepper

Rub

2	teaspoons Lawry's® Seasoned Salt
1	teaspoon granulated onion
1	teaspoon granulated garlic
1/2	teaspoon freshly ground black pepper

2   tablespoons spicy brown mustard

2   cups hickory chips, soaked in water for at least 30 minutes

1. In a medium bowl, combine the marinade ingredients. Put the steaks in a large, resealable plastic bag and pour in the marinade. Marinate at room temperature for 20 to 30 minutes.

2. In a medium bowl, combine the butter ingredients and mash with the back of a fork to distribute the seasoning evenly. Set aside at room temperature.

3. In a small bowl mix the rub ingredients.

4. Remove the steaks from the bag and discard the marinade. Spread the mustard over both sides of the steaks. Season evenly with the rub.

5. Drain the hickory chips and scatter them on the coals (or, if using a gas grill, place them in a smoker box).

6. With the lid closed, sear the steaks over ***direct medium*** heat (400°F to 450°F) for 1 minute on each side. Then grill the steaks over ***indirect medium*** heat until cooked to desired doneness, 4 to 5 minutes for medium-rare, turning once. Remove from the grill and let rest for 2 to 3 minutes before cutting into 1/4-inch slices. Smear the topside with the butter. Serve warm.

Makes 4 to 6 servings

Isaac's Inspiration

FROM
SERGEANT ISAAC GONZALEZ, MCB QUANTICO
1ST RUNNER UP

Paste

1/4	cup Jack Daniel's® whiskey
1/4	cup Kikkoman® Teriyaki Marinade & Sauce
3	tablespoons olive oil
3	tablespoons fresh orange juice
3	tablespoons finely chopped fresh parsley
3	tablespoons finely chopped fresh cilantro
	Juice of 1 lime
1	garlic clove
4	New York strip steaks, about 8 ounces each and 3/4 inch thick

Rub

1	teaspoon sea salt
1/2	teaspoon freshly ground black pepper
1/2	teaspoon Goya® Adobo seasoning
1/2	teaspoon Goya® Sazon seasoning
	Olive oil

1. In a blender combine the paste ingredients. Process until you have a smooth paste.

2. Smear the paste over both sides of each steak. Cover and refrigerate for 2 to 4 hours.

3. In a small bowl mix the rub ingredients.

4. Wipe most of the marinade off the steaks. Lightly coat both sides of each steak with oil. Season evenly with the rub. Let the steaks stand at room temperature for 20 to 30 minutes before grilling.

5. With the lid closed, grill the steaks over *direct high* heat (500°F to 550°F) until cooked to desired doneness, 5 to 7 minutes for medium-rare, turning once. (If flare-ups occur, move the steaks temporarily over *indirect high* heat.) Remove from the grill and let rest for 2 to 3 minutes. Serve warm.

Makes 4 servings

Marinated Rib-Eye Steaks with Onions and Mushrooms

FROM
MASTER SERGEANT BILLY KNOWLES, MCB QUANTICO
2ND RUNNER UP

Marinade

2	tablespoons Crown Royal® whiskey
2	tablespoons extra virgin olive oil
1	tablespoon minced garlic
1	teaspoon kosher salt
1/2	teaspoon freshly ground black pepper
4	rib-eye steaks, 10 to 12 ounces each and about 1 inch thick

Vegetables

1	tablespoon unsalted butter
1	tablespoon extra virgin olive oil
1/2	cup thinly sliced yellow onions
2	cups thinly sliced button mushrooms
1	tablespoon Kikkoman® Teriyaki Marinade & Sauce

1. In a small bowl mix the marinade ingredients.

2. Brush the marinade evenly over both sides of the steaks. Let the steaks stand at room temperature for 20 to 30 minutes before grilling. Meanwhile, cook the vegetables.

3. Heat a large skillet over medium-high heat. Add the butter and oil together. When the butter has melted, add the onions and cook for 2 minutes, stirring occasionally. Add the mushrooms and cook until the vegetables are tender, 4 to 6 minutes, stirring often. Add the teriyaki sauce and stir to combine. Remove the pan from the heat and grill the steaks.

4. With the lid closed, grill the steaks over *direct high* heat (500°F to 550°F) until cooked to desired doneness, 6 to 8 minutes for medium-rare, turning once. (If flare-ups occur, move the steaks temporarily over *indirect high* heat.) Let rest for 2 to 3 minutes. Meanwhile reheat the vegetables over medium-high heat. Serve the steaks warm with the vegetables spooned over the top.

Makes 4 servings

Rosemary-Crusted Filet Mignon Steaks with Gorgonzola Sauce

FROM
KEN NORTON

Rub

2	teaspoons finely chopped fresh rosemary
2	teaspoons kosher salt
1	teaspoon freshly ground black pepper
1	teaspoon grated orange zest
1	teaspoon dried fennel seed
4	filet mignon steaks, about 8 ounces each and 1-1/4 inches thick
	Extra virgin olive oil

Sauce

3 to 4	ounces shallots (about 4)
	Extra virgin olive oil
1/4	teaspoon kosher salt
1/4	teaspoon freshly ground black pepper
1/2	cup dry white wine
1/4	cup freshly squeezed orange juice
2	ounces Gorgonzola or other blue-veined cheese
1	teaspoon finely chopped fresh rosemary

1. Using a spice grinder or mortar and pestle, grind all the rub ingredients until the fennel seed is broken into tiny pieces.

2. Lightly coat the steaks on both sides with oil. Season evenly with the rub. Let stand at room temperature for 20 to 30 minutes before grilling.

3. Trim the root ends of the shallots and remove all the outer papery skin. Brush or spray with oil and season with the salt and pepper. Wrap loosely in aluminum foil. With the lid closed, grill the foil packet over **direct medium** heat (400°F to 450°F) until shallots are soft when pierced with the tip of a knife, 20 to 30 minutes, turning once. Remove from the grill and allow the shallots to cool slightly. Meanwhile, in a small heavy-bottomed saucepan, bring the wine and orange juice to a simmer over medium-high heat. Reduce the liquid to about 1/3 cup, 10 to 12 minutes. Remove from the heat. Roughly chop the cooled shallots. Add the shallots and the remaining sauce ingredients to the saucepan. Stir to incorporate the cheese, mashing it slightly to help with melting.

4. With the lid closed, grill the steaks over **direct medium** heat until cooked to desired doneness, about 10 minutes for medium-rare, turning once or twice.

5. Just before serving, warm the sauce over low heat sauce (do not boil). Spoon the sauce over the steaks. Serve immediately.

Makes 4 servings

Ken Norton

In 1973, the 6' 2", 220-pound Ken Norton made boxing history when he met Muhammad Ali for the heavyweight title, and won.

During the height of his boxing career, Norton was screen-tested and won the role in Dino De Laurentis' film, *"Mandingo."* This was later followed by a second film, *"Drum,"* both of which were international hits. On September 9, 1973, Norton was awarded the internationally famed Napoleon Hill Award for being an "outstanding positive thinker." Norton was the first athlete and the first African American to receive the honor.

Ken believes in pushing himself to the limit and being the best that he can possibly be. Growing up in Jacksonville, Illinois, boxing was not one of Norton's early interests. He earned a football, basketball, and track scholarship to Northeast Missouri State College, and it wasn't until he enlisted in the Marine Corps that Ken was introduced to boxing. In time, Ken became the best boxer to ever fight for the Marine Corps, and was awarded the North Carolina AAU Golden Gloves, International AAU, and Pan American titles. Later Ken was inducted into the Marine Corps Sport Hall of Fame.

Ken became a Corporal in the Marine Corps.

MCB CAMP LEJEUNE
MCAS NEW RIVER

Captain Eric "Disco" Dominijanni

Captain Eric Peter Dominijanni is a born-and-raised New Yorker whose passion since childhood has been cooking. In Iraq, in the initial march into Baghdad during Operation Iraqi Freedom and Operation Enduring Freedom, he brought along his espresso maker and he even made paella for his troops in the back of his Assault Amphibian vehicle. "I may have had to fight like a barbarian, but I didn't have to eat like one," Captain Dominijanni said.

In this, his signature recipe for steak, he combines the sweetness of cola with the pungency of garlic, the tanginess of lemon and orange zest, and the spiciness of habanero pepper in a marinade that will have your taste buds doing a Captain D dance.

As for the final competition ahead in New York City, Dominijanni says, "I've been dreaming of this since I was 7 years old. I cannot wait to go home for this." To his challengers he warns, "Gentlemen, you are in my house, my territory, so be prepared to go up against a guy who was born and raised in New York and knows exactly what everyone wants to eat over there. You're on my turf, gents. Oorah."

Disco's Hot and Tangy New York Strip Steaks

FROM
CAPTAIN ERIC "DISCO" DOMINIJANNI
MCB CAMP LEJEUNE

Marinade

1	can (12 ounces) cola
1/2	cup soy sauce
1/2	cup garlic teriyaki sauce
1	habanero chile pepper, finely chopped with seeds
1	tablespoon grated orange zest
1	tablespoon freshly ground ginger
1	tablespoon extra virgin olive oil
1	teaspoon freshly ground black pepper
3/4	teaspoon fresh lemon juice
1/8	teaspoon kosher salt

4	New York strip steaks, about 8 ounces each and 3/4 inch thick
	Extra virgin olive oil

1. In a medium bowl mix the marinade ingredients. Place the steaks in a large, resealable plastic bag and pour in the marinade. Press out the air, seal the bag, and turn several times to coat the meat. Place the bag in a bowl and refrigerate for 4 to 6 hours, turning the bag occasionally.

2. Let the steaks stand at room temperature for 20 to 30 minutes before grilling. Remove the steaks from the bag and reserve the marinade. Pour the marinade into a small saucepan, bring to a boil, and boil for about 10 seconds. Set aside about half of the marinade for basting the steaks. For the remaining marinade in the saucepan, reduce the heat to a simmer and cook until it has reduced to the consistency of a dipping sauce, 5 to 10 minutes, stirring occasionally. Set aside.

3. Pat the steaks dry with paper towels. Lightly coat the steaks with oil.

4. With the lid closed, grill the steaks over **direct high** heat (500°F to 550°F) until cooked to desired doneness, 5 to 7 minutes for medium-rare, turning once and basting with a little of the boiled marinade. (If flare-ups occur, move the steaks temporarily over *indirect high* heat.) Remove from the grill and let rest for 2 to 3 minutes. Serve warm with the dipping sauce on the side.

Makes 4 servings

Carl's Bodacious Caribbean Style T-Bone Steaks

FROM
SERGEANT MAJOR CARL H. RODRIGUEZ, MCAS NEW RIVER
1ST RUNNER UP

Rub

2	teaspoons dried cilantro
2	teaspoons minced onion flakes
1-1/2	teaspoons granulated garlic
1-1/2	teaspoons dried parsley
1-1/2	teaspoons Lawry's® Seasoned Salt

4	T-bone steaks, 12 to 16 ounces each and about 1 inch thick
	Vegetable oil
1	teaspoon McCormick® Caribbean Jerk Seasoning
1/3	cup favorite barbecue sauce

1. In a small bowl mix the rub ingredients.

2. Lightly coat the steaks on both sides with oil. Season evenly with the rub, pressing the spices into the meat. Cover with plastic wrap and refrigerate for 1 hour. Let the steaks stand at room temperature for 20 to 30 minutes before grilling.

3. Immediately before grilling, season the steaks evenly with the jerk seasoning. With the lid closed, grill over **direct high** heat (500°F to 550°F) until cooked to desired doneness, 6 to 8 minutes for medium-rare, turning once or twice and brushing with the barbecue sauce. (If flare-ups occur, move the steaks temporarily over *indirect high* heat.) Remove the steaks from the grill and let rest for 2 to 3 minutes. Serve warm.

Makes 4 to 6 servings

Gunny's T-Bone Steaks

FROM
GUNNERY SERGEANT CHARLES BROWN, MCB CAMP LEJEUNE
2ND RUNNER UP

Paste

1/4	cup (1/2 stick) sweet butter, softened
1	tablespoon minced garlic
1	tablespoon minced fresh cilantro
1	teaspoon minced fresh sage
1	teaspoon sea salt
1	teaspoon freshly ground black pepper

4	T-bone steaks, about 16 ounces each and 1 inch thick

1. In a small bowl, mash the paste ingredients with the back of a fork, and then stir to distribute the seasonings throughout the paste.

2. Let the steaks stand at room temperature for 20 to 30 minutes before grilling.

3. Use your fingertips to rub the paste evenly over both sides of the steaks. Continue to spread the paste over the meat until the paste looks like a thin veil over the red flesh (clumps of butter would create flare-ups).

4. With the lid closed, grill the steaks over **direct high** heat (500°F to 550°F) until cooked to desired doneness, 6 to 8 minutes for medium-rare, turning once. (If flare-ups occur, move the steaks temporarily over *indirect high* heat.) Remove from the grill and let rest for 2 to 3 minutes. Serve warm.

Makes 4 to 6 servings

Country Style Rib-Eye Steaks with Tennessee Spices

FROM
GEORGE JONES

4	bone-in rib-eye steaks, about 12 ounces each and 1 inch thick
1	cup George Jones Barbeque Marinade
	Extra virgin olive oil

Rub

1	teaspoon paprika
1	teaspoon kosher salt
1/2	teaspoon granulated garlic
1/2	teaspoon dark brown sugar
1/2	teaspoon dried thyme
1/2	teaspoon freshly ground black pepper

1. Place the steaks in a large, plastic resealable bag and pour in the marinade. Press out the air, seal the bag, and turn several times to coat the meat. Place the bag in a bowl and refrigerate for 1-1/2 to 2 hours, turning the bag occasionally.

2. Remove the steaks from the bag and pour the marinade into a small saucepan. Heat the sauce over medium-high heat and let it boil for 10 seconds. Coat the steaks lightly on both sides with the oil.

3. In a small bowl mix the rub ingredients. Season the steaks evenly with the rub, pressing the spices into the meat. Let the steaks stand at room temperature for 20 to 30 minutes before grilling.

4. With the lid closed, grill the steaks over ***direct medium-high*** heat (450°F to 500°F) until cooked to desired doneness, 8 to 10 minutes for medium-rare, turning once and brushing with the boiled marinade. (If flare-ups occur, move the steaks temporarily over *indirect medium-high* heat.) Transfer to a cutting board and let rest for 3 to 5 minutes. Carve the meat from the bone and cut the steak across the grain into 1/4-inch slices, discarding any large pieces of fat. Arrange the slices on a platter or individual plates. Drizzle any juices collected on the cutting board over the slices. Serve warm.

Makes 4 to 6 servings

George Jones

George Jones first hit the charts in 1955 with "Why, Baby, Why."

Jones has won numerous awards throughout his career beginning in 1956 as *Billboard* magazine's "Most Promising New Country Vocalist" to country music's ultimate recognition—his 1992 induction into the Country Music Hall of Fame. In 2002 he was awarded the National Medal of Arts Honor for artistic excellence. Jones has won two Grammys—separated by eighteen years—the first in 1981 and the second in 1999.

Mr. Jones recently celebrated his fiftieth anniversary as a recording artist with the release of a three CD set entitled *George Jones 50 Years of Hits*, which featured one hit for each year of his career.

George Jones was a Private First Class while in the Marine Corps.

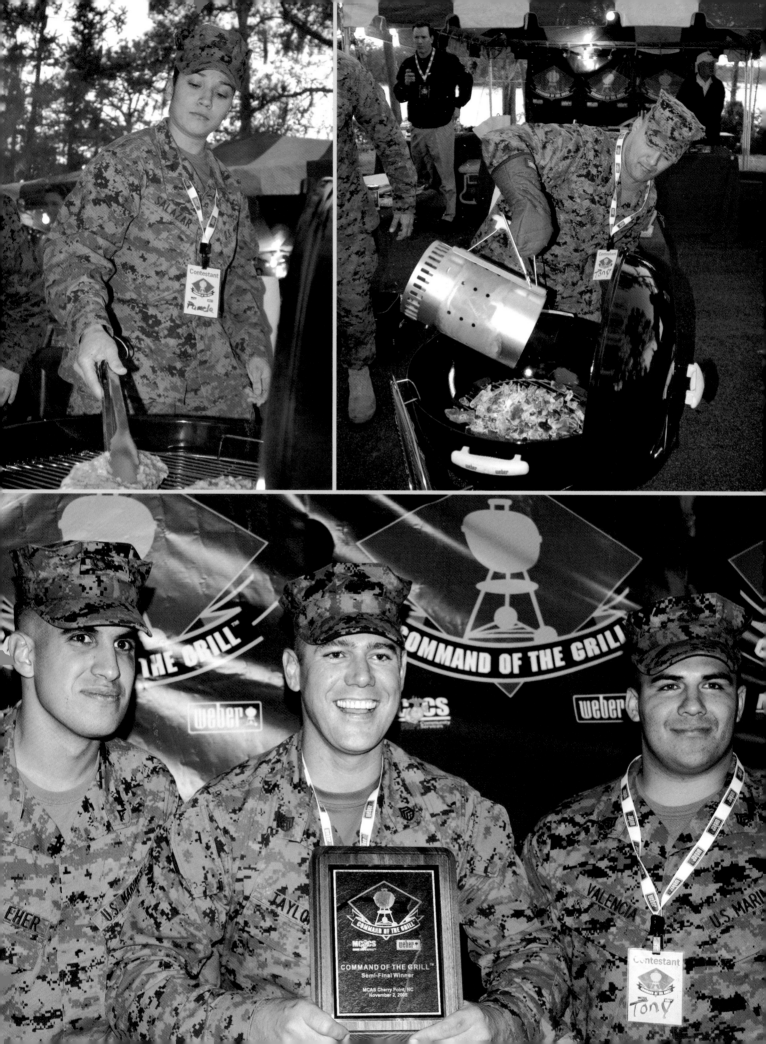

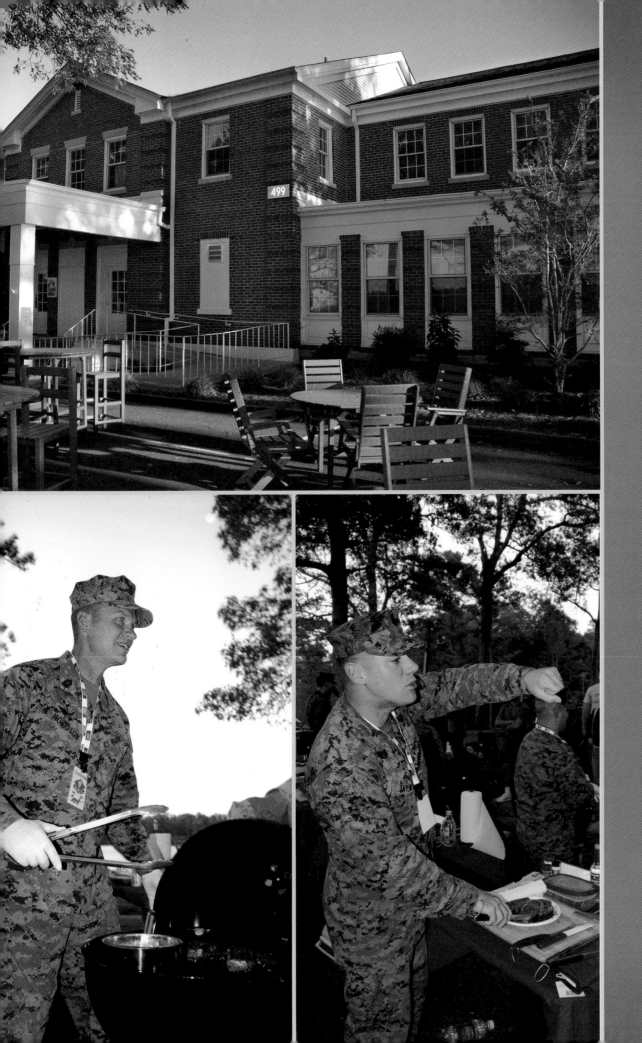

Staff Sergeant Joseph Taylor

Staff Sergeant Joseph Taylor is an Aviation Ordinance Technician who was born and raised in North Carolina. Throughout his 17-year career in the Marine Corps, Taylor has been stationed all over the United States and overseas and "anywhere you can probably imagine." When he's not building bombs for the Marines, Taylor loves to grill with friends and family. He added, "I'm from North Carolina… we grill anything…we're always grilling!"

Taylor took inspiration for his Command of the Grill™ recipe from, of all things, sushi. "I made a rub using wasabi powder, ginger, and a few other items and it came out real good." So good, that during Halloween, Taylor passed out little pieces of steak to the parents of the trick-or-treaters that came to his house. His recipe got rave reviews from the whole neighborhood.

While he claims he will make some slight adjustments to his original recipe, Taylor feels that he has a great chance to win the grand prize, and the ensuing bragging rights. With his fellow Marines and family rooting him on in New York City, he'll be ready for the heated competition with hopes of being named Master and Commander of the Grill.

Tremendous Teriyaki Steak

FROM
STAFF SERGEANT JOSEPH TAYLOR
MCAS CHERRY POINT

1 flank steak, 1-1/2 to 2 pounds and about 3/4 inch thick, trimmed of any surface fat

2 cups sake
1/2 cup soy sauce
1 tablespoon brown sugar

Rub
2 teaspoons sesame seed
1 teaspoon ground ginger
1 teaspoon wasabi powder
1 teaspoon granulated garlic
1 teaspoon freshly ground black pepper
1/2 teaspoon kosher salt

 Vegetable oil

---

1. Put the steak in a large, plastic resealable bag. Add the sake, soy sauce, and brown sugar. Press the air out of the bag, seal tightly, and turn several times to distribute the sake. Refrigerate for about 1 hour.

2. In a small bowl mix the rub ingredients.

3. Remove the steak from the bag, allowing the excess liquid to drip off. Coat the steak lightly on both sides with oil. Season evenly with the rub, pressing the spices into the meat. Let the steak stand at room temperature for 20 to 30 minutes before grilling.

4. With the lid closed, grill the steak over ***direct high*** heat (500°F to 550°F) until cooked to desired doneness, 8 to 10 minutes for medium-rare, turning once. Remove from the grill and let rest for about 5 minutes before cutting crosswise (against the grain) into thin strips. Serve warm.

Makes 4 to 6 servings

Valencia Mexican Steaks

FROM
Sergeant Antonio Valencia, MCAS Cherry Point
1ST RUNNER UP

Marinade

1	cup roughly chopped fresh cilantro
1/2	cup fresh orange juice
1/2	cup Corona® Extra beer
2	tablespoons fresh lime juice
2	tablespoons vegetable oil
1	tablespoon cider vinegar
1	teaspoon kosher salt
1	teaspoon dried oregano
1/2	teaspoon pure chile powder
1/2	teaspoon freshly ground black pepper

4	T-bone steaks, 12 to 16 ounces each and about 1 inch thick
1	medium orange, cut in half

1. In a medium bowl mix the marinade ingredients.

2. Put the steaks in a large, resealable plastic bag and pour in the marinade. Press out the air, seal the bag tightly, and turn the bag several times to distribute the marinade evenly. Refrigerate for 2 to 4 hours.

3. Remove the steaks from the bag and discard the marinade. Let the steaks stand at room temperature for 20 to 30 minutes before grilling. Just before putting the steaks on the grill, squeeze the juice from the orange halves over the steaks.

4. With the lid closed, grill the steaks over *direct high* heat (500°F to 550°F) until cooked to desired doneness, 6 to 8 minutes for medium-rare, turning once. (If flare-ups occur, move the steaks temporarily over *indirect high* heat.) Remove from the grill and let rest for 2 to 3 minutes. Serve warm.

Makes 4 to 6 servings

Fire in the Hole Strip Steaks

FROM
Lance Corporal Christopher J. Kelleher, MCAS Cherry Point
2ND RUNNER UP

Marinade

	Finely grated zest and juice of 1 orange
	Finely grated zest and juice of 1 lemon
	Finely grated zest and juice of 1 lime
6	garlic cloves, roughly chopped
2	jalapeño chile peppers, roughly chopped
1	serrano chile pepper, roughly chopped
1	yellow caribe chile pepper, roughly chopped
1/2	teaspoon freshly ground black pepper
1/4	teaspoon ancho chile powder
1/4	teaspoon chipotle chile powder
1/4	teaspoon ground cumin
1/4	teaspoon paprika
1/4	teaspoon sea salt

4	New York strip steaks, about 8 ounces each and 3/4 inch thick
1/2	cup olive oil
3	tablespoons roughly chopped fresh cilantro

1. Place the marinade ingredients into a blender. Process until smooth.

2. Put the steaks in a large, resealable plastic bag and pour in the marinade. Add the olive oil and cilantro. Press the air out of the bag and seal tightly. Turn the bag to distribute the marinade, place in a bowl, and refrigerate for 2 hours, turning occasionally.

3. Let the steaks stand at room temperature for 20 to 30 minutes (in the bag) before grilling. Remove the steaks from the bag and discard the marinade. With the lid closed, grill the steaks over *direct high* heat (500°F to 550°F) until cooked to desired doneness, 5 to 7 minutes for medium-rare, turning once. (If flare-ups occur, move the steaks temporarily over *indirect high* heat.) Remove the steaks from the grill and let rest for 2 to 3 minutes before carving. Sprinkle the cilantro evenly over the steaks. Serve warm.

Makes 4 servings

Garlic and Balsamic-Marinated Steaks with Rosemary

FROM
BUM PHILLIPS

Marinade

3	tablespoons extra virgin olive oil
1	tablespoon balsamic vinegar
2	teaspoons Dijon mustard
2	teaspoons minced fresh rosemary
2	teaspoons minced garlic
1	teaspoon kosher salt
1/2	teaspoon celery seed
1/4	teaspoon freshly ground black pepper

4	New York strip steaks, 10 to 12 ounces each and about 3/4 inch thick
1/2	teaspoon kosher salt
1/4	teaspoon freshly ground black pepper
2	large sprigs (4 to 6 inches long) fresh rosemary (optional)

1. In a medium bowl mix the marinade ingredients.

2. Brush the marinade evenly over both sides of the steaks. Cover and refrigerate for 4 to 6 hours. Let the steaks stand at room temperature for 20 to 30 minutes before grilling.

3. Just before grilling, season the steaks evenly with the remaining salt and pepper. If using a charcoal grill, toss the rosemary sprigs over the coals for smoke. With the lid closed, grill the steaks over *direct medium-high* heat (450°F to 500°F) until cooked to desired doneness, 8 to 10 minutes for medium-rare, turning once or twice. (If flare-ups occur, move the steaks temporarily over *indirect medium-high* heat.) Remove from the grill and let rest for 2 to 3 minutes. Serve warm.

Makes 4 servings

Bum Phillips

Born Oail A. Phillips Jr. in Orange, Texas, Bum got his nickname from his older sister who could not pronounce "brother."

Mr. Phillips' football coaching career began in Nederland, Texas, in 1950 and includes a total of thirteen years at the high school level, six years in college, and seventeen years in the National Football League—eleven as head coach and general manager for which he gained the most notoriety.

Bum Phillips was named head coach and general manager of the Houston Oilers in 1975. Although the Oilers had won just eight games in the prior three seasons, Bum was able to raise the franchise to a perennial play-off contender with three consecutive play-off appearances in 1978, 1979, and 1980.

Appointed head coach and general manager of the New Orleans Saints in 1981, Phillips moved to Louisiana where he brought the Saints back into the game. After five years there, Bum retired from football and moved back home to Texas to pursue his first love—ranching.

He and his wife Debbie have six children, twenty-three grandchildren, and two great-grandchildren. His son, Wade, is the defensive coordinator of the San Diego Chargers.

Bum Phillips was a Private in the Marine Corps.

CAMP ALLEN

Staff Sergeant Jeremiah E. Batista

Staff Sergeant Jeremiah Batista has served in the Marine Corps for nearly 10 years and is a Combat Load Specialist. While stationed in Guantanamo Bay, Cuba, Batista and his fellow troops would pull out the grill every chance they got. When asked why he entered the Command of the Grill™ contest, Batista replied, "I got such great reviews about my cooking while in Cuba, I said, 'what the heck, let me try this contest and I'll see how good I really am.'"

Batista developed a Caribbean-style sauce for his winning steak recipe, inspired by his dad. Batista's love for grilling can be traced back three generations, with chefs, restaurant owners, and culinary students in his family. His sage grilling advice, "When you're grilling out there, don't go too heavy on salt."

Looking ahead to the New York finals, Batista is going to stick with his original winning recipe, "I think it will stand on its own," he said. Not only will he be competing for his fellow Marines at Camp Allen in the finals, Batista claims he wants to win the grand prize in order to present a new grill to his dad. "It would be a gift from me to him for inspiring me with the recipe."

Presidente Steak

FROM
Staff Sergeant Jeremiah E. Batista
Camp Allen

Marinade

2	cups dark beer, at room temperature
1/2	cup roughly chopped yellow onion
1/3	cup fresh lemon juice
1	tablespoon kosher salt
1	tablespoon minced garlic
1	tablespoon dried oregano
4	T-bone steaks, 12 to 16 ounces each and about 1 inch thick
	Extra virgin olive oil

1. In a large, resealable plastic bag set inside a bowl, combine the marinade ingredients.

2. Add the steaks to the bag. Press the air out of the bag, seal tightly, and turn several times to distribute the ingredients. Marinate the steaks at room temperature for 20 to 30 minutes before grilling, turning the bag occasionally. Remove the steaks from the marinade, reserve the marinade, and pat the steaks dry with paper towels. Lightly coat the steaks with oil on both sides. Pour the marinade into a saucepan, bring to a boil over medium-high heat, and boil for about 10 seconds.

3. With the lid closed, grill the steaks over *direct high* heat (500°F to 550°F) until cooked to desired doneness, 6 to 8 minutes for medium-rare, turning once or twice and basting with some of the boiled marinade. (If flare-ups occur, move the steaks temporarily over *indirect high* heat.) Remove from the grill and let rest for 2 to 3 minutes. Serve warm.

Makes 4 to 6 servings

McGruff's Own

FROM
GUNNERY SERGEANT SEAN P. MCFADDEN, CAMP ALLEN
1ST RUNNER UP

3	tablespoons extra virgin olive oil
1	tablespoon Morton & Bassett® Italian Seasoning
1	teaspoon kosher salt
1/2	teaspoon freshly ground black pepper
4	New York strip steaks, 8 to 10 ounces each and about 3/4 inch thick

1. In a small bowl mix the oil, Italian seasoning, salt, and pepper.

2. Coat the steaks on both sides with the seasoned oil mixture. Let the steaks stand at room temperature for 20 to 30 minutes before grilling.

3. With the lid closed, grill the steaks over **direct high** heat (500°F to 550°F) until cooked to desired doneness, 5 to 7 minutes for medium-rare, turning once. (If flare-ups occur, move the steaks temporarily over *indirect high* heat.) Remove the steaks from the grill and let rest for 2 to 3 minutes. Serve warm.

Makes 4 servings

Sweet Success

FROM
1ST SERGEANT DAVID PELLEY, CAMP ALLEN
2ND RUNNER UP

Marinade

1/3	cup juice from canned baked beans
1/3	cup fresh orange juice
1/4	cup A-1® Steak Sauce
1/4	cup fresh lime juice
1	tablespoon granulated sugar
4	rib-eye steaks, 10 to 12 ounces each and about 1 inch thick
	Extra virgin olive oil
1	teaspoon kosher salt
1/4	teaspoon freshly ground black pepper

1. In a medium bowl mix the marinade ingredients until the sugar is dissolved.

2. Place the steaks into a large, resealable plastic bag and pour in the marinade. Press out the air, seal the bag tightly, and turn the bag several times to distribute the marinade evenly. Refrigerate for 30 to 60 minutes.

3. Remove the steaks from the bag and discard the marinade. Lightly coat the steaks on both sides with oil. Season evenly with the salt and pepper. Let the steaks stand at room temperature for 20 to 30 minutes before grilling.

4. With the lid closed, grill the steaks over **direct medium** heat (400°F to 450°F) until cooked to desired doneness, 8 to 10 minutes for medium-rare, turning once. (If flare-ups occur, move the steaks temporarily over *indirect medium* heat.) Remove from the grill and let rest for 2 to 3 minutes. Serve warm.

Makes 4 servings

Flatiron Steaks
with Salsa Verde

FROM
LEE TREVINO

Sauce

3/4	cup loosely packed fresh Italian parsley leaves and tender stems
1/4	cup loosely packed fresh cilantro leaves and tender stems
2	teaspoons rinsed capers
1	medium garlic clove
6	tablespoons extra virgin olive oil
1	tablespoon red wine vinegar
1	teaspoon finely chopped jalapeño chile pepper, with seeds
	Kosher salt
	Freshly ground black pepper

4	flatiron steaks, each about 8 ounces and 1/2 inch thick
	Extra virgin olive oil
1	teaspoon kosher salt
1/2	teaspoon freshly ground black pepper

1. In a food processor, finely chop the parsley, cilantro, capers, and garlic. With the motor running, add the oil, vinegar, and jalapeño. Stop the motor and scrape down the sides of the bowl. Process again until you a have a fine puree that can be spooned over meat. Add salt and pepper to taste.

2. Lightly coat the steaks on both sides with oil. Season evenly with the salt and pepper. Let the steaks stand at room temperature for 20 to 30 minutes before grilling. With the lid closed, grill the steaks over ***direct high*** heat (500°F to 550°F) until cooked to desired doneness, 5 to 7 minutes for medium-rare, turning once or twice. Remove from the grill and let rest for 2 to 3 minutes. Meanwhile, stir the sauce so it has an even consistency. Cut the steaks across the grain into 1/2-inch slices and serve warm with the sauce drizzled over the top.

Makes 4 servings

Lee Trevino

Lee Trevino's biggest thrill was winning the 1971 U.S. Open in Oak Hill. In a four-week period that year, Trevino won three of golf's prestige competitions—the U.S. Open, the Canadian Open, and the British Open.

Raised next door to the Glen Lake Country Club in Dallas, Trevino got started as a caddy. Self-taught as a youth, he became the protégée of Hardy Greenwood. In 1960 he got his first job working as an assistant professional in El Paso, Texas.

Despite a freak accident in which Trevino was struck by lightning at the Western Open, he eventually lifted the U.S. PGA trophy in 1984, much to the surprise of the golfing community.

Trevino served in the Marine Corps for four years from age seventeen to twenty-one. He left as a Lance Corporal. In 2001 Trevino was inducted into the Marine Corps Sport Hall of Fame.

Sergeant Michael Clawson

Sergeant Michael Clawson joined the Marines in 1994. A reservist who works as a Heavy Machine Gunner, he entered the Command of the Grill™ contest with few expectations of winning. As a "kid from Salt Lake City" in a town known for barbecue (Kansas City), he really never thought he'd go home with grilling honors. But, he says, he won "because his steak tasted like it's supposed to."

When developing his recipe for the competition, Clawson tried to recreate "the flavor of the Western mountains." Hailing from Utah, he spent a lot of time in the great outdoors fishing, camping, and hunting. Sage and rosemary grew wild on the hillsides near where he lived, and was a favorite food of elk and other game in the area. "The flavor of the sage and rosemary comes through subtly in the meat of the elk," he remarked. Since contest rules prohibited him from grilling steaks from an elk he hunted and butchered himself, he decided to try to create the same rosemary-sage flavor in his beef steak recipe.

Clawson has some advice for those who might want to try their hand at grilling elk. "It cooks fast, and because it has a low fat content, it can dry out quickly," he warns. "Grill it over low heat for a short amount of time."

Sergeant Clawson said he "had a blast" competing in the semi-finals and is looking forward to the finals in New York City. To prepare, he plans to sleep-in late, get plenty of rest, and not get too nervous. "I'm going to New York to have fun."

Steak Fajitas with Rocky Mountain Rub

FROM
SERGEANT MICHAEL CLAWSON
MOBCOM KANSAS CITY

2   skirt steaks, about 1 pound each and 3/4 inch thick

Marinade
3   tablespoons extra virgin olive oil
1   tablespoon balsamic vinegar
1   tablespoon minced garlic
1   teaspoon Worcestershire sauce

Guacamole
2   ripe Hass avocados
1   tablespoon finely chopped fresh cilantro
2   teaspoons fresh lime juice
1   teaspoon minced garlic
1/2 teaspoon kosher salt
1/4 teaspoon freshly ground black pepper

Rub
1   teaspoon dried sage
1   teaspoon dried rosemary
1/2 teaspoon dried oregano
1/2 teaspoon kosher salt
1/4 teaspoon celery salt
1/4 teaspoon freshly ground black pepper

1   medium red onion, sliced crosswise into 1/3-inch slices
2   medium red or green bell peppers, seeded and cut into flat sections
     Extra virgin olive oil
8   flour tortillas, each 8 inches in diameter

1. With a fork, poke each side of each steak 3 or 4 times to allow the marinade to seep inside the meat. In a small bowl mix the marinade ingredients.

2. Brush the marinade evenly over both sides of each steak. Let the steaks stand at room temperature for 20 to 30 minutes before grilling.

3. In a medium bowl, combine the guacamole ingredients and stir with a fork until thoroughly combined. Cover the surface with plastic wrap until ready to use.

4. In a small bowl combine the rub ingredients and crush them between your fingertips to release the oils in the herbs. Just before grilling, brush the garlic off the steaks and then season the steaks on both sides with the rub, pressing the spices into the meat.

5. Lightly brush or spray the onion and bell peppers on both sides with oil. With the lid closed, grill the onion, bell peppers, and steaks over *direct high* heat (500°F to 550°F) until the veggies are tender and the steaks are cooked to desired doneness, turning once. The onion will take 8 to 10 minutes, the bell peppers will take 6 to 8 minutes, and the steaks will take 5 to 7 minutes for medium-rare. Remove from the grill and let the steaks rest for 2 to 3 minutes. Cut the onion and bell peppers into bite-sized pieces. Wrap the tortillas in a foil packet. With the lid down, grill the packet over *direct medium* heat (400°F to 450°F) to warm the tortillas, about 2 to 3 minutes, turning once.

6. To serve, cut the skirt steak against the grain into 1/4 inch slices. Place the warm tortillas, sliced meat, onions, peppers, and guacamole in separate serving dishes. Let each person make their own fajita by placing the fillings down the center of each tortilla. Wrap and serve warm.

Makes 4 servings

Thompson's Steaks

FROM
SERGEANT KEITH THOMPSON, MOBCOM KANSAS CITY
1ST RUNNER UP

4   New York strip steaks, 10 to 12 ounces each and about 3/4 inch thick
Extra virgin olive oil

1-1/2 teaspoons kosher salt

1   teaspoon granulated garlic

1   teaspoon freshly ground black pepper

2   tablespoons unsalted butter, softened, cut in 4 equal pieces

1. One at a time, place each steak between 2 sheets of plastic wrap and use a meat tenderizer or the bottom of a heavy saucepan to pound it to a thickness of about 1/2 inch. Trim off any excess fat along the outer edges of each steak. Lightly coat the steaks with oil on both sides. Season evenly with the salt, granulated garlic, and pepper. Let the steaks stand at room temperature for 20 to 30 minutes before grilling.

2. With the lid closed, grill the steaks over **direct high** heat (500°F to 550°F) until cooked to desired doneness, 5 to 7 minutes for medium-rare, turning once. (If flare-ups occur, move the steaks temporarily over *indirect high* heat.) Remove the steaks from the grill. Smear the butter evenly over the top side of each steak. Let the steaks rest for 2 to 3 minutes. Serve warm.

Makes 4 servings

Teriyaki Surprise

FROM
MASTER GUNNERY SERGEANT HAROLD LANG, MOBCOM KANSAS CITY
2ND RUNNER UP

2   cups Kikkoman® Teriyaki Marinade & Sauce

2   medium yellow onions, roughly chopped

1   lemon, thinly sliced

4   T-bone steaks, 12 to 16 ounces each and about 1 inch thick
Vegetable oil

1   teaspoon Lawry's® Seasoned Salt

1   teaspoon lemon pepper

1. In a large, resealable plastic bag combine the teriyaki sauce, onions, and lemon. Add the steaks to the bag. Press out the air, seal the bag tightly, and turn the bag several times to evenly distribute the marinade. Refrigerate for about 1 hour.

2. Remove the steaks from the bag and reserve the marinade. Pat the steaks dry with paper towels and lightly coat with oil on both sides. Season evenly with the seasoned salt and lemon pepper. Let the steaks stand at room temperature for 20 to 30 minutes before grilling. Meanwhile pour the marinade into a medium saucepan. Bring to a boil over medium-high heat and boil for about 10 seconds.

3. With the lid closed, grill the steaks over **direct high** heat (500°F to 550°F) until cooked to desired doneness, 6 to 8 minutes for medium-rare, turning once or twice and brushing with a little of the boiled marinade. (If flare-ups occur, move the steaks temporarily over *indirect high* heat.) Remove from the grill and let rest for 2 to 3 minutes. Serve warm.

Makes 4 to 6 servings

Sirloin Steak with Roasted Pepper Salsa

FROM
JO JO WHITE

Salsa

3	slices yellow onion, each 1/2 inch thick
	Olive oil
1	large yellow bell pepper
1	cup diced (1/2 inch) ripe tomato
1	tablespoon finely chopped fresh cilantro
1	tablespoon fresh lime juice
1/4	teaspoon kosher salt
1/4	teaspoon freshly ground black pepper
1/8	teaspoon Tabasco® sauce, or more to taste

Rub

2	teaspoons paprika
2	teaspoons dark brown sugar
2	teaspoons kosher salt
1/2	teaspoon freshly ground black pepper
1	top sirloin steak, 1-1/2 to 2 pounds and about 1 inch thick
	Olive oil

1. Lightly coat the onion slices on both sides with oil. With the lid closed, grill the bell pepper and onion slices over *direct medium-high* heat (450°F to 500°F). Grill the bell pepper until the skin is blackened and blistered in spots, 12 to 15 minutes, turning 3 or 4 times. Grill the onion slices until well marked and tender, 8 to 10 minutes, turning once. Place the pepper in a small bowl and cover with plastic wrap to trap the steam. Set aside for at least 10 minutes, and then peel away the charred skin. Cut off the top and remove the seeds. Dice the pepper into 1/2-inch pieces. Dice the onion slices into 1/2-inch pieces. In a medium bowl combine the bell peppers and onions with the remaining salsa ingredients. Add 1 tablespoon of olive oil. Mix well.

2. In a small bowl mix the rub ingredients.

3. Lightly coat the steak on both sides with oil. Season evenly with the rub, pressing the spices into the meat. Let the steak stand at room temperature for 20 to 30 minutes before grilling.

4. With the lid closed, grill the steak over *direct medium-high* heat (450°F to 500°F) until cooked to desired doneness, 8 to 10 minutes for medium-rare, turning once or twice. Remove from the grill and let rest for 3 to 5 minutes. Cut the steak into thick slices and spoon the salsa over the top.

Makes 4 to 6 servings

Jo Jo White

Jo Jo White, a consummate professional basketball player, was such a dynamic and gifted all-around athlete that the Dallas Cowboys and the Cincinnati Reds both drafted him. White, however, chose basketball and the Celtics.

A major highlight of White's career occurred on June 4, 1976, at the Boston Garden in Game 5 of the NBA Championship Finals against the Phoenix Suns. White led the Celtics with 33 points spread out over 60 minutes in the 128-126 triple-overtime victory. That season, he was crowned the NBA Finals Most Valuable Player.

White may have invented the term, "ironman streak," in the NBA. From the 1972-73 season through the 1976-77 campaign, five consecutive seasons, White played in all 82 regular season games for the Celtics—such stats are unheard of today. For seven straight seasons White logged more than 3200 minutes per season. He was named to the NBA All-Star Team each of those seven years. The Boston Celtics later retired his number 10 jersey.

Mr. White remains with the Celtics organization, serving as Director of Special Projects and Community Relations Representative. He continues to remain an active member of the National Basketball Retired Players Association.

From June 1969-1976 Jo Jo White was a Private First Class in the Marine Corps.

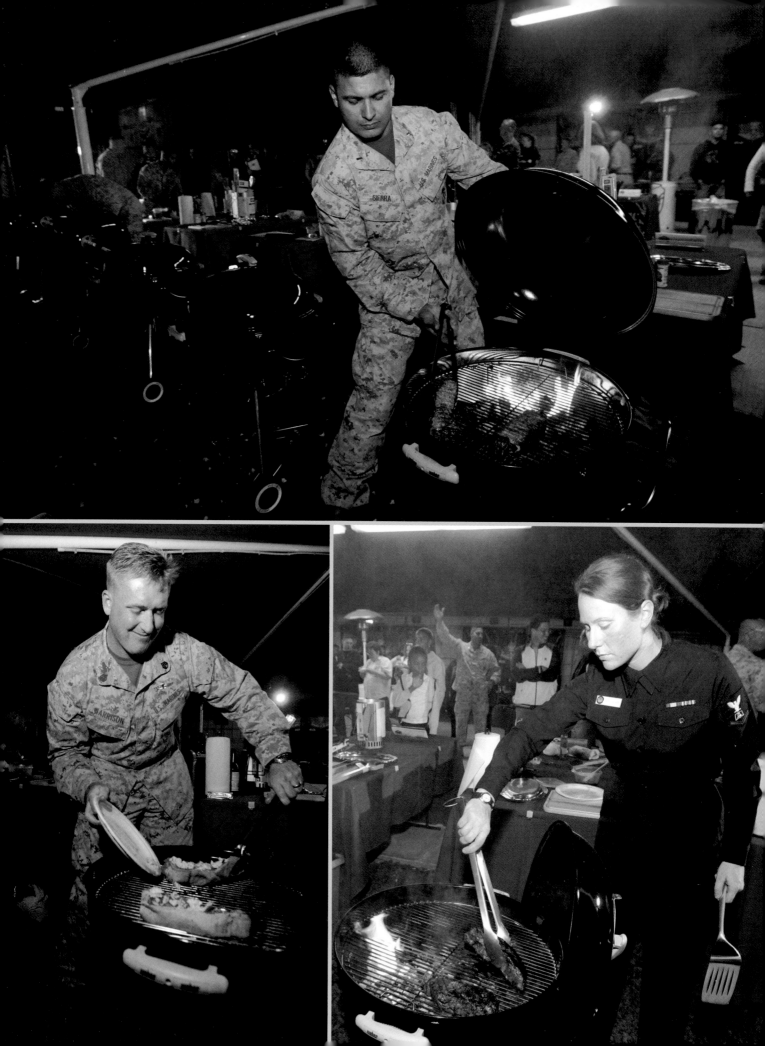

MCAGCC 29 PALMS

Captain Phillip Woodward

Captain Phillip Woodward is a Maintenance Officer who has been in the Marine Corps for almost 22 years. "Yeah, I've been just about everywhere you can go. I've been to the Philippines, Iraq, Kuwait, Japan, Korea, Thailand, Australia, Norway, France, England, Europe, South America, and then just about every state in the United States."

He entered the Command of the Grill™ contest because, he said, "I think I cook a good steak." Inspired by his brother-in-law at an early age, Woodward claims to have always been interested in grilling. His advice for a great tasting steak, "Try and get the meat as tender as possible. That's what a marinade does for you. Lemon juice is the real key. Then throw in a little brown sugar and a bit of soy sauce, those kinds of things, for flavor."

With several Ironman triathlons under his belt, Woodward is always training for another race. He eats a steak every Sunday night in order to protein load, which he says, improves his recovery time from his weekend training.

In the final competition, Woodward plans on using every second of the time allotted to make sure his steaks are marinated to perfection. "As long as I don't mess up the cooking time for the steaks, I don't see how you can cook it any better."

Spud's Grilled Steaks

FROM
CAPTAIN PHILLIP WOODWARD
MCAGCC 29 PALMS

Marinade

1	cup soy sauce
1/2	cup olive oil
1/4	cup finely chopped yellow onion
2	large garlic cloves, peeled and crushed
1	tablespoon Mrs. Dash® Original Blend
1	tablespoon fresh lemon juice
1	teaspoon granulated garlic
1	teaspoon granulated onion
1/2	teaspoon Worcestershire sauce
1/4	teaspoon brown sugar
1/4	teaspoon freshly ground black pepper

4	porterhouse steaks, 12 to 16 ounces each and about 1 inch thick
1	teaspoon Mrs. Dash® Original Blend

---

1. In a large, resealable plastic bag set inside a large bowl, combine the marinade ingredients. Poke the steaks all over with a fork and add the steaks to the bag. Press the air out of the bag and seal tightly. Turn the bag several times to distribute the marinade, place the bag back in the bowl, and refrigerate for 30 to 60 minutes.

2. Remove the steaks from the bag and reserve the marinade. Let the steaks stand at room temperature for 20 to 30 minutes before grilling. Meanwhile, pour the marinade into a medium saucepan. Bring to a boil over medium-high heat and boil for about 10 seconds.

3. With the lid closed, grill the steaks over ***direct medium-high*** heat (450°F to 500°F) until cooked to desired doneness, 8 to 10 minutes for medium-rare, turning once or twice and brushing with a little of the boiled marinade. (If flare-ups occur, move the steaks temporarily over *indirect medium-high* heat.) Remove from the grill, sprinkle the Mrs. Dash over the steaks and let rest for 2 to 3 minutes before slicing. Serve warm.

Makes 4 to 6 servings

Jeff's Sizzling Sirloin Steaks

FROM
CHIEF WARRANT OFFICER 2 JEFFREY D. CARMENIA, MCAGCC 29 PALMS
1ST RUNNER UP

Marinade

1/4	cup extra virgin olive oil
2	tablespoons Worcestershire sauce
1	tablespoon fresh lemon juice
1	tablespoon finely chopped fresh rosemary
2	teaspoons balsamic vinegar
1	teaspoon granulated garlic
1	teaspoon kosher salt
1	teaspoon freshly ground black pepper
4	sirloin steaks, 10 to 12 ounces each and about 1-1/4 inches thick

1. In a small bowl mix the marinade ingredients.

2. Place the steaks in a large, plastic resealable bag and pour in the marinade. Press the air out of the bag and seal it tightly. Turn the bag several times to distribute the marinade evenly. Refrigerate for 1 to 2 hours. Remove the steaks from the bag and discard the marinade. Let the steaks stand at room temperature for 20 to 30 minutes before grilling.

3. With the lid closed, grill the steaks over ***direct medium*** heat (400°F to 450°F) until cooked to desired doneness, 12 to 15 minutes for medium-rare, turning once. Remove from the grill and let rest for 2 to 3 minutes before slicing. Serve warm.

Makes 4 to 6 servings

Bistec Rojo de Ajo

FROM
SERGEANT JENNIE HASKAMP, MCAGCC 29 PALMS
2ND RUNNER UP

Butter

1/4	cup (1/2 stick) unsalted butter, melted
2	teaspoons freshly ground black pepper
2	packets or 2 teaspoons Sazón Goya® with Coriander and Annatto
1-1/2	teaspoons red wine vinegar
1	teaspoon minced garlic
4	T-bone steaks, 12 to 16 ounces each and about 1 inch thick

1. In a small bowl mix the butter ingredients.

2. Pierce the steaks 6 to 8 times on each side with a fork. Lightly brush the butter mixture over both sides of the steaks. Let the steaks stand at room temperature for 20 to 30 minutes before grilling.

3. With the lid closed, grill the steaks over ***direct medium-high*** heat (450°F to 500°F) until cooked to desired doneness, 8 to 10 minutes for medium-rare, turning once or twice and brushing with the remaining butter mixture. (If flare-ups occur, move the steaks temporarily over *indirect medium-high* heat.) Remove the steaks from the grill and let them rest for 2 to 3 minutes. Serve warm.

Makes 4 to 6 servings

Red Wine-Marinated Steaks with Sun-Dried Tomato Butter

FROM
TOM SEAVER

Marinade

2	cups dry red wine
1/4	cup balsamic vinegar
1/4	cup extra virgin olive oil
8	medium garlic cloves, roughly chopped
3	tablespoons roughly chopped fresh basil
2	teaspoons crushed red pepper flakes
2	teaspoons kosher salt
1	teaspoon freshly ground black pepper

4   New York strip or rib-eye steaks, about 10 ounces each and 1 inch thick

Butter

1/4	cup sun-dried tomatoes packed in oil, drained
1/2	cup (1 stick) unsalted butter, softened
1/2	teaspoon kosher salt
1/4	teaspoon freshly ground black pepper

1. In a medium bowl mix the marinade ingredients.

2. Place steaks in a large plastic, resealable bag. Pour the marinade into the bag, press out the air, seal the bag, and turn several times to coat the steaks. Place the bag in a bowl and refrigerate for 1 to 2 hours, turning the bag occasionally.

3. To prepare the butter, put the sun-dried tomatoes in a food processor or blender. Process until smooth. Place the butter in a small bowl. Add the sun-dried tomatoes, salt, and pepper to the butter. Blend until the ingredients are evenly distributed.

4. Remove the steaks from the bag and discard the marinade. Pat the steaks dry with paper towels and let stand at room temperature for 20 to 30 minutes before grilling. With the lid closed, grill the steaks over **direct high** heat (500°F to 550°F) until cooked to desired doneness, 6 to 8 minutes for medium-rare, turning once or twice. Let the steaks rest at room temperature for 3 to 5 minutes before serving warm with a spoonful of butter on top of each one.

Makes 4 servings

Tom Seaver

George Thomas Seaver was born in Fresno, California. He became known as the franchise power pitcher who transformed the New York Mets from losers into a team to be reckoned with.

The quintessential professional, Seaver won 311 games with a 2.86 ERA over twenty seasons and his 3,272 strikeouts set a National League career record. Seaver fanned 3,640 batters in his career, including two hundred or more ten times, and once struck out nineteen in a single game. "Number 41" was the National League Rookie of the Year in 1967, a three-time Cy Young Award winner, and made more Opening Day starts, sixteen, than any pitcher in history. The Baseball Writers Association of America elected Seaver to the National Baseball Hall of Fame in 1992.

During his formidable career, Tom Seaver played for the New York Mets (1967-1977, 1983), Cincinnati Reds (1977-1982), Chicago White Sox (1984-1986), and the Boston Red Sox (1986). Other important dates include: 1969 NLCS, 1969 World Series, 1973 NLCS, 1973 World Series, 1979 NLCS and was selected to play in thirteen All-Star Games in 1967-1973, 1975-1978, 1981.

"He's so good that blind people come to the park just to hear him pitch," said Reggie Jackson.

Tom Seaver was a Private First Class in the Marine Corps. He was inducted into the Marine Corps Sport Hall of Fame in 2003.

Biography facts courtesy of Baseball Hall of Fame.

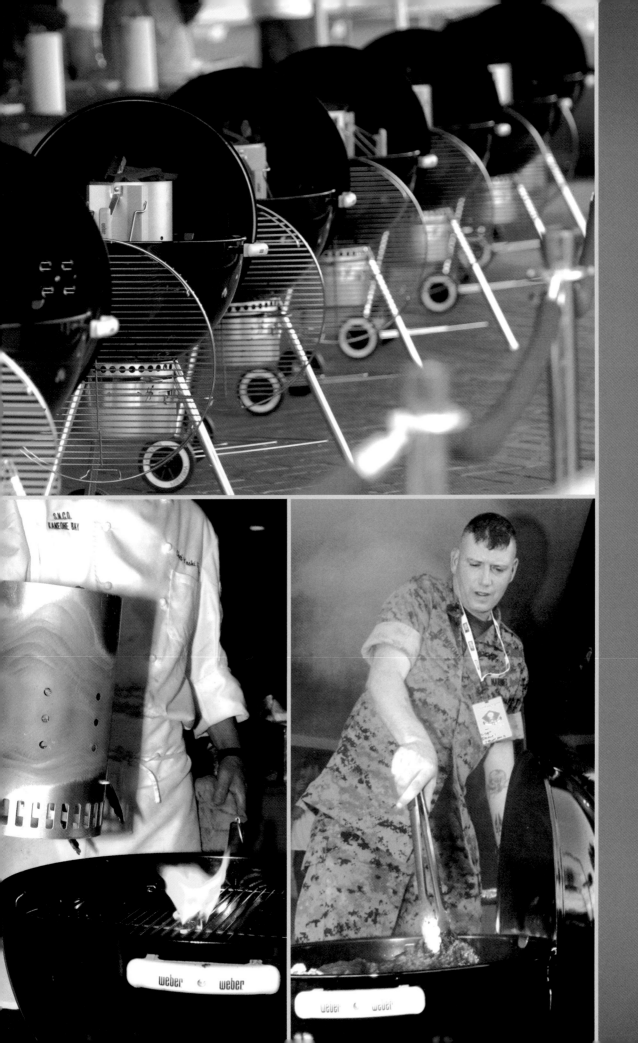

Staff Sergeant Daniel G. Newcomb

Staff Sergeant Daniel Newcomb is a Postal Chief with 14 years of service in the Marine Corps. At the age of 17, Newcomb learned to grill while working as a line cook at a steakhouse in Omaha, Nebraska. He quickly became an expert at cooking steaks, hamburgers, and other cuts of meat. "I learned how to get something a certain way like medium-rare, how much of a certain ingredient you use with it, what to look for while you're cooking it," he said.

This basic training in grilling steak paid off for him at the competition held at the Marine Corps Base in Kaneohe Bay, Hawaii. Newcomb used his skills to create a recipe that featured toasted sesame seeds in the marinade. The sesame seeds, he says, give it a different flavor than you would find in other marinades.

Since he won the competition he's continued to tinker with his recipe, perfecting it in hopes of bringing home the title of Command of the Grill Grand Champion. "I feel like I did my best job at the competition, but there's always room to improve," he stated. "I'm going to keep practicing and see how well I do."

Portabello Mushroom Steak

FROM
STAFF SERGEANT DANIEL G. NEWCOMB
MCB HAWAII

Marinade

2	cups soy-based barbecue sauce
1/2	cup light brown sugar
1/2	cup roughly chopped yellow onion
1/2	cup roughly chopped green bell pepper
1/4	cup toasted sesame seed

1	top sirloin steak, 1-1/2 to 2 pounds and about 1-1/4 inches thick
2	medium portabello mushrooms
1	medium green bell pepper, stemmed and seeded
1	small yellow onion
1/4	cup light olive oil, divided
2	teaspoons freshly ground black pepper, divided
1/4	teaspoon kosher salt

---

1. In a medium bowl mix the marinade ingredients, reserving 1 tablespoon of the marinade for the vegetable packet.

2. Place the steak in a 2-inch-deep rectangular dish and pour the marinade over the steak. Set aside at room temperature for 30 minutes, turning over the steak occasionally. Meanwhile, prepare the vegetables.

3. Remove the mushroom stems and discard. Wipe the mushroom caps with a damp paper towel. With a teaspoon, scrape out the dark gills and discard. Cut each mushroom in half, and then cut each half crosswise into 1/3-inch slices. Cut the bell pepper lengthwise into 1/3-inch strips. Cut the onion in half through the stem and root ends, then cut each half lengthwise into 1/4-inch slices. In a medium bowl mix the mushrooms with the bell peppers, onions, 2 tablespoons of the oil, 1 tablespoon of the marinade, 1/4 teaspoon of the pepper, and the salt. Mix gently. Place the mushroom mixture on a sheet of aluminum foil (about 18 inches by 18 inches). Pull up the corners of the foil and seal the packet tightly.

4. Remove the steak from marinade, allowing the excess liquid to drip off and discard the marinade. Lightly coat the steak on both sides with the remaining 2 tablespoons of oil. Season the steak evenly with the remaining pepper. With the lid closed, grill the steak over *direct high* heat (500°F to 550°F) until cooked to desired doneness, 8 to 10 minutes for medium-rare, turning once or twice. (If flare-ups occur, move the steaks temporarily over *indirect high* heat.) At the same time, grill the packet of vegetables over *direct high* heat until the vegetables are tender, 8 to 10 minutes, turning the packet once.

5. Remove the steak from grill and let rest for about 5 minutes. Carefully open the packet of vegetables (**watch for steam**). Cut the steak into thick slices and serve the steak with the vegetables spooned over the top.

Makes 4 servings

Hawaiian Island Barbecue Beef

FROM
GUNNERY SERGEANT STEVEN BURKETT, MCB HAWAII
1ST RUNNER UP

Sauce

1	large head garlic
	Vegetable oil
2	slices fresh pineapple, each 1/2 inch thick, cored
1/2	cup ketchup
1/4	cup distilled white vinegar
2	tablespoons molasses
1	tablespoon Sriracha chili sauce
1/2	teaspoon kosher salt
1/4	teaspoon freshly ground black pepper
1	tri-tip roast, about 2 pounds and 1-1/2 inches thick
	Vegetable oil
1	teaspoon kosher salt
1/2	teaspoon freshly ground black pepper

1. Remove the loose, papery outer skin from the head of garlic. Using a sharp knife, cut about 1/2 inch off the top to expose the cloves. Place the garlic head on a large square of heavy-duty aluminum foil and drizzle 1 tablespoon of oil over the top of the cloves. Fold up the foil sides and seal to make a packet, leaving a little room for the expansion of steam. With the lid closed, grill over **indirect medium** heat (400°F to 450°F) until the pulp is golden brown and tender, 45 minutes to 1 hour. Set aside to cool. Squeeze the pulp from the garlic into a blender.

2. Lightly coat the pineapple slices on both sides with oil. With the lid closed, grill over **direct medium** heat (400°F to 450°F) until well marked and tender, 8 to 10 minutes, turning once. Roughly chop the pineapple and add to the blender. Add the remaining sauce ingredients. Process until smooth.

3. Lightly coat the roast with oil on all sides. Season evenly with the salt and pepper, pressing the spices into the meat. Let the meat stand at room temperature 20 to 30 minutes before grilling.

4. With the lid closed, grill the meat over **direct medium** heat until well marked on 2 sides, about 10 minutes, turning once. Move the meat over **indirect medium** heat and grill, with the lid closed, until cooked to desired doneness, about 15 minutes more for medium-rare, brushing the meat generously with the sauce on all sides (you will not need all of it) and turning it over every 5 minutes or so. Transfer the meat to a cutting board, lightly cover with foil, and let rest for 5 to 10 minutes. Cut the meat across the grain into very thin slices. Serve warm with the remaining sauce.

Makes 6 servings

Steak Satay

FROM
MAJOR KEVIN McCOULLOUGH, MCB HAWAII
2ND RUNNER UP

Marinade

1/4	cup soy sauce
1/4	cup rice vinegar
1/4	cup olive oil
2	tablespoons dark brown sugar
1	tablespoon dark sesame oil
1	tablespoon fresh lemon juice
1	tablespoon minced garlic
1	teaspoon grated ginger
1/2	teaspoon red pepper flakes
1	flank steak, 1-1/2 to 2 pounds and about 3/4 inch thick

1. In a small bowl mix the marinade ingredients until the sugar is dissolved.

2. Cut the flank steak crosswise and at a 45-degree angle into 1/2-inch slices. Each strip should be 4 to 6 inches long. Thread the flank steak slices onto skewers, keeping the meat as flat as possible. Lay the skewers of beef in a dish just large enough to hold them and the marinade. Pour the marinade over the beef. Turn the skewers to distribute the marinade evenly. Marinate the meat at room temperature for 20 to 30 minutes.

3. Lift the skewers from the marinade and let the marinade drip off. Discard the marinade. With the lid closed, grill the meat over **direct high** heat (500°F to 550°F) until lightly charred on the surface but still juicy in the center, 3 to 5 minutes, turning once. Serve warm.

Makes 4 servings

Note: If using bamboo skewers, soak them for at least 1 hour in water first to prevent the skewers from burning.

Garlic-Studded Steaks with Anaheim Chiles

FROM

WILFORD BRIMLEY

8	small garlic cloves
4	bone-in rib-eye steaks, about 16 ounces each and 2 inches thick
1	teaspoon Lawry's® Seasoned Salt
1	teaspoon coarsely ground black pepper
1/2	teaspoon ground cayenne pepper

Salsa

2	tablespoons unsalted butter
1	cup finely chopped yellow onions
2/3	cup finely chopped Anaheim chile peppers
1/2	cup thinly sliced green onions

1. Cut each garlic clove in half lengthwise. Use the tip of a small knife to cut 4 narrow slits in each steak. Stuff the garlic into the slits. In a small bowl mix the seasoned salt, black pepper, and cayenne pepper. Season the steaks evenly with the spices. Let the steaks stand at room temperature for 20 to 30 minutes before grilling. Meanwhile make the salsa.

2. In a medium skillet melt the butter over medium-high heat. Add the yellow onions, chile peppers, and green onions. Mix well. Cook until the onions are golden brown and tender, 4 to 6 minutes, stirring occasionally.

3. With the lid closed, sear the steaks over **_direct high_** heat (500°F to 550°F) until well marked on each side, 8 to 10 minutes, turning once (if flare-ups occur, move the steaks temporarily over _indirect high_ heat). Finish cooking the steaks over **_indirect high_** heat until cooked to desired doneness, 8 to 10 minutes for medium-rare, turning once. Remove from the grill and let rest for 3 to 5 minutes before cutting the steaks into 3/4-inch slices. Spoon the salsa over the slices. Drizzle any juices collected on the cutting board over the top. Serve warm.

Makes 4 to 6 servings

Wilford Brimley

Wilford Brimley is well known for his performances in _The Firm, Absence of Malice,_ and _Cocoon_. He is also familiar to television audiences from his appearances in a long-running series of Quaker Oats commercials and is currently doing an endorsement for Liberty Medical.

He is also known for starring in the family-oriented television series, _Our House._

Other notable performances include a nuclear plant employee in _The China Syndrome_ (1979), _The Electric Horseman_ (1979), _The Thing_ (1982), _Tender Mercies_ (1983), _Country, The Natural, The Stone Boy, Hotel New Hampshire_ (all 1984), and a leading role in _End of the Line_ (1987).

From 1953-56 Wilford Brimley proudly served in the United States Marine Corps and was honorably discharged as Sergeant.

MCAS BEAUFORT

MCRD PARRIS ISLAND

Sergeant Michael Clayton

When he's not working with explosives and demolitions, Sergeant Michael Clayton is definitely taking command of the grill. A Combat Engineer who has been in the Marine Corps for 4 years, Clayton's experience includes front-line duty in Iraq as well as Kuwait.

Clayton is a self-taught griller who has continued to master his craft with the philosophy of trial and error. During the Command of the Grill™ contest he decided to keep his recipe sweet and simple, as his Sensational Southern Steaks won him top honors in Beaufort, South Carolina. His recipe involves rubbing the steak with garlic salt, and then combining it with a half and half mixture of Dale®'s Steak Seasoning and Dr. Pepper®. "Really, really simple..." said Clayton.

Equally experienced in charcoal and gas grilling, Clayton should be a tough competitor in New York. When asked about his plan for the finals, he claims that he will stick with his original recipe due to its success in South Carolina. With the support of his fellow Marines, as well as the help of some friends who have graduated from culinary school, Clayton will be looking to take home the grand prize.

Sensational Southern Steaks

FROM
SERGEANT MICHAEL CLAYTON
MCRD PARRIS ISLAND

4	filet mignon steaks, 8 to 10 ounces each and about 1-1/2 inches thick
	Extra virgin olive oil
1	teaspoon garlic salt
2	teaspoons Dale®'s Steak Seasoning
2	teaspoons Dr. Pepper®

1. Lightly coat the steaks with oil. Season evenly with the garlic salt. Drizzle the Dale's seasoning and Dr. Pepper all over the steaks.

2. Let the steaks stand at room temperature for 20 to 30 minutes before grilling. With the lid closed, grill the steaks over **direct medium** heat (400°F to 450°F) until cooked to desired doneness, 12 to 15 minutes for medium-rare, turning once. Let rest for 2 to 3 minutes. Serve warm.

Makes 4 servings

Clark's Marinated Steaks

FROM
SERGEANT DONALD CLARK, MCRD PARRIS ISLAND
1ST RUNNER UP

Marinade

3	tablespoons Worcestershire sauce
1	tablespoon A-1® Steak Sauce
1	tablespoon melted butter
1	tablespoon minced garlic
1	teaspoon Morton & Bassett® Italian Seasoning
1/2	teaspoon paprika
1/2	teaspoon kosher salt
1/2	teaspoon freshly ground black pepper
1/8	teaspoon ground cayenne pepper

4	rib-eye steaks, 10 to 12 ounces each and about 1 inch thick

1. In a medium bowl mix the marinade ingredients.

2. Smear the marinade over both sides of the steaks. Let the steaks stand at room temperature for 20 to 30 minutes before grilling.

3. With the lid closed, grill the steaks over *direct high* heat (500°F to 550°F) until cooked to desired doneness, 6 to 8 minutes for medium-rare, turning once. (If flare-ups occur, move the steaks temporarily over *indirect high* heat.) Remove from the grill and let rest for 2 to 3 minutes. Serve warm.

Makes 4 servings

Filet Mignon Steaks
with Hollandaise Sauce

FROM
ART DONOVAN JR.

6	filet mignon steaks, each about 8 ounces and 1 inch thick
	Extra virgin olive oil
1	teaspoon kosher salt
1/2	teaspoon freshly ground black pepper

Sauce

3	large egg yolks
1/2	cup (1 stick) unsalted butter, melted and cooled to room temperature
1	tablespoon fresh lemon juice
	Kosher salt

1. Lightly coat the steaks on both sides with oil. Season evenly with the salt and pepper. Let the steaks stand at room temperature for 20 to 30 minutes before grilling. Meanwhile, make the sauce.

2. Whisk the egg yolks in the upper section of a double boiler. Add 2 tablespoons of water to the egg and whisk again. Pour 1 to 2 inches of hot water in the bottom section of the double boiler and put the upper section in place. Whisking often, slowly bring the water in the bottom section to a simmer. Do not let the water boil. When the egg mixture is as thick as heavy cream, drizzle the melted butter very, very slowly into the egg mixture, whisking constantly. After all the butter has been incorporated, add the lemon juice and remove the double boiler from the heat. Add salt to taste.

3. Grill the steaks over ***direct high*** heat (500°F to 550°F) until cooked to desired doneness, 6 to 8 minutes for medium-rare, turning once. Remove the steaks from the grill and let rest for 2 to 3 minutes. Serve warm with the sauce spooned over the top.

Makes 6 servings

Art Donovan Jr.

Arthur Donovan Jr., football giant extraordinaire, was born in Bronx, New York, and graduated from Boston College. Donovan, the defensive tackle in the "greatest game ever played"—1958 NFL Championship Game where the Baltimore Colts defeated the New York Giants, 23-17, in overtime—was unstoppable for more than a decade.

On the field, his 265 pounds and 6' 2" frame intimidated the opposition, but his smile and star personality attracted fans by the thousands.

Donovan joined the National Football League's Baltimore Colts in 1950. The team moved in 1951 to become the New York Yanks and relocated again in 1952 to become the Dallas Texans. The team returned "home" in 1953 as the Baltimore Colts. During his twelve-year tenure in the pros, Art Donovan was named Outstanding Defensive Tackle. Between 1953-1957, he was chosen to play in five Pro Bowl games plus the World Championships in 1958 and 1959. In 1962 the Colts retired Art's uniform, number 70, when he departed from pro football. Five years later, he became the first Baltimore Colt to receive the sport's grandest honor—membership in the Pro Football Hall of Fame.

Art's father, Arthur Donovan, was a very prominent boxing referee. He refereed 21 of Joe Louis's fights plus many others. He served in WWI and WWII plus the Mexican Border War. Art's grandfather, Mike O'Donovan, was middleweight champion of the world and served in the Civil War.

Art Donovan Jr. spent three years in military service during World War II with the United States Marine Corps as a Private First Class. In 2004 he was inducted into the Marine Corps Sport Hall of Fame.

MCAS YUMA

Lance Corporal Jaynine Goodroe

As a girl growing up in the small town of Lapeer, Michigan, Lance Corporal Jaynine Goodroe was inspired by ads she saw on TV about being a Marine. After graduating from high school, she enlisted and is now a Personnel Administrator stationed in Yuma, Arizona.

Jaynine learned the art of grilling from her dad, who was an avid charcoal griller. "He'll come up with any reason to cook and he'll grill anything," she says. "I've seen him grill all kinds of vegetables and he's even grilled hot wings."

With the smoke of the charcoal fire in her blood, Goodroe quickly signed-up for the competition when she saw a flyer for the Command of the Grill™ competition on a station bulletin board. On the day of the competition, she not only was one of the lowest ranking Marines in the grill-off, she also was the only woman competing.

She wowed the judges with her recipe, which she says she created by taking a little inspiration from several different recipes she liked. But she says the real secret was marinating the steak in lemon juice, a trick she learned from her mother. "My mom taught me that a little lemon juice will actually tenderize your steak. So I went ahead and used a little lemon juice."

Her parents are excited about her advancing to the finals. "My dad has taken a lot of credit for me winning this competition. He said I definitely got it from him. Mom's pretty happy, too. She wants to buy a ticket and go with me to New York to support me," Goodroe said.

When she competes in the finals in New York City, Goodroe will again be the only woman manning the grill. "I had never realized that grilling was a male dominated sport," she said. "It just makes me want to try even harder."

Rib-Eye Steaks with Mediterranean "Marine-ade"

FROM
LANCE CORPORAL JAYNINE GOODROE
MCAS YUMA

Marinade

1/2	cup dry red wine
1/4	cup olive oil
2	tablespoons fresh lemon juice
1	teaspoon dried marjoram
1	teaspoon dried thyme
1	teaspoon garlic salt
1	teaspoon crushed red pepper flakes
4	rib-eye steaks, 10 to 12 ounces each and about 1 inch thick
1	teaspoon garlic salt

1. In a large, plastic resealable bag set inside a large bowl, combine the marinade ingredients. Add the steaks to the bag. Press the air out of the bag and seal tightly. Turn the bag several times to distribute the marinade, place the bag back in the bowl, and marinate for 30 to 60 minutes.

2. Remove the steaks from the bag and let the excess liquid drip off. Discard the marinade. Let the steaks stand at room temperature for 20 to 30 minutes before grilling. Just before grilling, season both sides of each steak with the garlic salt.

3. With the lid closed, grill the steaks over **direct high** heat (500°F to 550°F) until cooked to desired doneness, 6 to 8 minutes for medium-rare, turning once. (If flare-ups occur, move the steaks temporarily over *indirect high* heat.) Remove from the grill and let rest for 2 to 3 minutes. Serve warm.

Makes 4 servings

New York Strip Steaks with Ancho Chile Sauce

FROM
STAFF SERGEANT CHARLES DINE, MCAS YUMA
1ST RUNNER UP

Sauce

3	medium dried ancho chile peppers, stemmed, seeded, torn into pieces
3	large poblano chile peppers
1/2	cup half and half
1	tablespoon granulated sugar
2	teaspoons fresh lime juice
	Kosher salt
	Freshly ground black pepper
4	New York strip steaks, about 8 ounces each and 3/4 inch thick
2	tablespoons minced garlic
2	teaspoons Hawaiian sea salt
1	teaspoon ground cumin
1	cup Dos Equis® beer
1/2	cup finely chopped fresh cilantro
2	teaspoons cracked black peppercorns
2	tablespoons unsalted butter, softened

1. In a medium bowl combine the ancho peppers with 2 cups of hot water. Let stand until the peppers soften, about 30 minutes. Drain the peppers, reserving the soaking liquid. Meanwhile, with the lid closed, grill the poblano peppers over *direct medium* heat (400°F to 450°F) until blackened and blistered all over, 10 to 12 minutes, turning occasionally. Place the peppers in a paper bag; close tightly. Let stand for 10 to 15 minutes to steam off the skins. Remove the peppers from the bag and peel away the charred skins. Cut off the tops and remove the seeds. Finely chop the peppers.

2. In a blender combine the drained ancho peppers, 1/2 cup of the reserved soaking liquid, the chopped poblano peppers, half and half, sugar, and lime juice. Puree until smooth, adding more soaking liquid by tablespoonfuls if the sauce is too thick. Season with salt and pepper to taste. Put the sauce into a small saucepan.

3. With a fork, poke each steak 4 to 5 times on each side to allow the seasoning to seep inside the meat. Rub each steak on each side with the garlic, salt, and cumin. Put the steaks in a large, resealable plastic bag. Add the beer and cilantro. Press the air out of the bag, seal tightly, and turn several times to distribute the seasonings. Refrigerate for 4 to 6 hours.

4. Let the steaks stand at room temperature (in the bag) for 20 to 30 minutes before grilling. Remove the steaks from the bag, allowing the excess liquid to drip off. Discard the beer mixture. Season the steaks evenly with the pepper. With the lid closed, grill the steaks over *direct high* heat (500°F to 550°F) until cooked to desired doneness, 5 to 7 minutes for medium-rare, turning once. Meanwhile, warm the sauce over medium heat. Remove the steaks from the grill, smear the butter over the tops, and let rest for 2 to 3 minutes. Serve warm with the sauce.

Makes 4 servings

Perfect Steaks

FROM
GUNNERY SERGEANT ADAM WILNER, MCAS YUMA
2ND RUNNER UP

Rub

8	teaspoons salt
3	teaspoons black or white pepper
2	teaspoons garlic powder
1	teaspoon ground cayenne pepper
4	New York strip steaks, 8 to 10 ounces each and about 3/4 inch thick

1. In a small bowl mix the rub ingredients.

2. Sprinkle the rub on both sides of the steak to your desired taste (you will not need all of it). Let the steaks stand at room temperature for 20 to 30 minutes before grilling. Store the unused rub in a tightly sealed jar for up to one year.

3. With the lid closed, grill the steaks over *direct high* heat (500°F to 550°F) until cooked to desired doneness, 5 to 7 minutes for medium-rare, turning once. (If flare-ups occur, move the steaks temporarily over *indirect high* heat.) Remove from the grill and let rest for 2 to 3 minutes. Serve warm.

Makes 4 servings

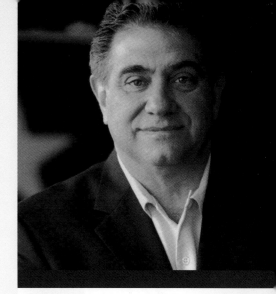

Marinated Flank Steak with Lemon-Garlic Butter

FROM
DAN LAURIA

Marinade

1/4	cup fresh lemon juice
1/4	cup extra virgin olive oil
1/4	cup roughly chopped fresh Italian parsley
4	medium cloves garlic, crushed
1	teaspoon crushed red chile flakes
1/2	teaspoon kosher salt

1	flank steak, 1-1/2 to 2 pounds and about 3/4 inch thick, trimmed of surface fat

Butter

1/3	cup unsalted butter, softened
1	tablespoon finely chopped fresh Italian parsley
1	teaspoon minced garlic
1	teaspoon finely grated lemon zest
1/4	teaspoon kosher salt
1/4	teaspoon freshly ground black pepper

1. In a medium bowl whisk the marinade ingredients. Pour the marinade into a large, resealable plastic bag and add the meat. Press out the air and seal the bag tightly, then turn the bag several times to distribute the marinade. Place the bag on a plate and refrigerate for 2 to 4 hours, turning the bag occasionally.

2. In a medium bowl mash the butter ingredients with the back of a fork and mix well to evenly distribute the seasonings.

3. Remove the steak from the marinade and discard the marinade. Let the steak stand at room temperature for 20 to 30 minutes before grilling. Grill the steak over **direct medium-high** heat (450°F to 500°F) until cooked to desired doneness, 8 to 10 minutes for medium-rare, turning once. Remove the steak from the grill and let rest for 3 to 5 minutes. Smear the lemon-garlic butter over the top. Cut the steak across the grain in thin slices. Serve warm.

Makes 4 to 6 servings

Dan Lauria

Dan Lauria is most recognized as the dad on the highly-acclaimed, Emmy-winning, ABC television show, *The Wonder Years*. He has guest starred in over seventy television episodic programs and boasts an impressive score of film credits, which include: *Stakeout, Another Stakeout, Independence Day,* and most recently, *Big Momma Two*.

In regional theatre, Mr. Lauria has performed in, written and/or directed over fifty productions. For ten years he served as the artistic director of the Playwright's Kitchen Ensemble of Los Angeles. With PKE, he produced over four hundred and fifty public readings of new plays with the finest actors in the business in order to promote the development of new American playwrights.

Serving in the Marine Corps from 1970 to 1973, Dan Lauria entered as a 2nd Lieutenant and left as a Captain.

Acknowledgements

Weber would like to thank the following companies for their generous support to this project:

United Airlines
www.united.com

Jeep
www.jeep.com

New York City Marriott Hotels
www.marriott.com

Smith & Wollensky
www.smithandwollensky.com

FCL Graphics
www.fclgraphics.com

Midland Paper
www.midlandpaper.com

Murnane Paper
www.murnanepaper.com

L&M Bindery

Platinum Converting
www.platinumconverting.com

Morrison Hotel Gallery
www.morrisonhotelgallery.com

Lobel's of New York
www.lobels.com

Bob Gruen
www.bobgruen.com